WILLIAMS-SONOMA

MASTERING

Hors d'Oeuvres

Author
JAN WEIMER

General Editor
CHUCK WILLIAMS

Photographer
BILL BETTENCOURT

NEW YORK · LONDON · TORONTO · SYDNEY

About this book

Mastering Hors d'Oeuvres offers every reader a cooking class in book form, a one-on-one lesson with a seasoned teacher standing by your side explaining each recipe step-by-step—with plenty of photographs to illustrate every detail.

Hors d'oeuvres serve an important purpose: to stimulate the appetites of your guests without overwhelming them, whether you are hosting a cocktail party or setting the stage for dinner. Hors d'oeuvres can be as simple as an herb-flecked bean dip or a bite of broiled chicken with peanut sauce, or as elaborate as scallop-edged tartlets or caviar-topped blini. In cooking your way through *Mastering Hors d'Oeuvres,* you will learn how to make these recipes and many others, and how to use your newly acquired skills to add creative finishing touches.

Here's how this book comprises a complete beginning course on hors d'oeuvres: In the opening pages, you'll find an overview of the different types of hors d'oeuvres and of the ingredients you use to make them. You'll also discover guidelines on choosing, cooking, and serving hors d'oeuvres. The Basic Recipes chapter includes two fundamental pastry doughs perfect for tartlets and turnovers. In addition, you will find recipes for a variety of canapé bases made from pita bread and baguettes, as well as homemade tortilla and potato chips—all of which can be served with a broad array of dips, spreads, and toppings. The Key Techniques chapter provides both photographs and instructions to teach you the important skills needed to excel in making hors d'oeuvres. Then comes a trio of recipe chapters: Dips & Spreads, Cold Hors d'Oeuvres, and Hot Hors d'Oeuvres.

Not only will you be able to put the skills you acquire in *Mastering Hors d'Oeuvres* to work in making appetizers for your family and friends, but you will also use them whenever you cook.

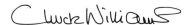

Working with the Recipes

Hors d'oeuvres are among the most highly anticipated elements of any gathering, whether you are hosting a casual afternoon get-together or an evening cocktail party. The carefully selected recipes in this book give you plenty of delicious hors d'oeuvres to choose from. And the practical way the recipes are organized will help you learn key culinary skills and then build on them, ensuring that your confidence grows each time you entertain.

The recipes in *Mastering Hors d'Oeuvres* cover a wide range: salsa and guacamole, tapenade and mushroom pâté, seafood tartares, bite-sized pastries, skewered vegetables and meats, and filo triangles. As you work your way through this book, keep in mind the importance of practice. The more hors d'oeuvres you make, the more proficient you will become. And even if your first attempts are not perfect, they will still be delicious.

Start by preparing the master recipes at the beginning of each chapter. Each one

includes detailed instructions and step-by-step photographs to guide you through every stage—as if you had a cooking teacher by your side. After practicing the master recipes, move on to the other recipes that follow. These recipes will also help you develop your skills and let you build your confidence gradually.

The many variations in each chapter will give you ideas for applying what you have learned to create a larger repertory of recipes by tailoring ingredients to suit your taste, the season, or the style of your

party. For example, once you've mastered Tuna Tartare with Lemon & Tarragon (page 83), you can trade the herbs, citrus juices, and vegetables for different seasonings in the variations that follow it. Similarly, the recipe for Chicken Skewers with Peanut Dipping Sauce (page 99) offers ideas for shrimp (prawns), beef, lamb, pork, vegetable, and fruit skewers, each with a unique sauce.

To find out more about the basic tools and equipment you will need to make hors d'oeuvres, turn to pages 132–35.

Types of Hors d'Oeuvres

Hors d'oeuvres fall into almost every culinary category, so it is complicated to divide them by how they are cooked. Instead, this book separates them into three chapters to help you pick a recipe well-suited to your event, whether you need a single recipe to serve as the first course before dinner or a balanced selection of recipes for a larger party. In the pages that follow, you will be selecting from dips and spreads, cold hors d'oeuvres, and hot hors d'oeuvres.

Dips & Spreads

Popular with guests and often simple to make, dips and spreads are perfect for entertaining. When served casually in attractive bowls surrounded by crudités (raw vegetables), chips, or toasts, they also make excellent icebreakers because they encourage guests to mingle. Most dips can also double as spreads for Toasts (page 22) or vegetable slices. For the most elegant presentation, spoon or pipe a dip into Toast Cups (page 22) and pass them on a platter.

Guacamole (page 60) paired with homemade Tortilla Chips (page 24) is always a welcome combination at casual get-togethers. Depending on the size of your group, consider adding White Bean Dip (page 51) or any of its variations (pages 56–57). Or, serve Tapenade (page 63) as a delicious prelude to a Mediterranean-style dinner party.

Think about the season when planning your menu, too. Mushroom Pâté (page 64) spread on small toasts makes an excellent appetizer for an autumn supper, while Salsa Fresca (page 59) is best in summer, when vine-ripe tomatoes are at their peak.

Cold Hors d'Oeuvres

When you want to serve such classic hors d'oeuvres as deviled eggs or stuffed cherry tomatoes, new potatoes, or endive leaves, turn to this chapter. One reason these recipes are classics is that many of them are easy for people to make ahead. You'll find other favorites here, too, such as Prosciutto-Wrapped Figs & Melon (page 92) or Honey-Glazed Spiced Nuts (page 95). For a more elegant offering, serve Oysters on the Half Shell with Mignonette Sauce (page 88) or try Tuna Tartare with Lemon & Tarragon (page 83) or one of its variations (page 85).

You will need to plan in advance for some of these recipes. For example, for Gravlax (page 87), you must start curing the salmon four days ahead of time. For blini, plan to make the batter early in the morning on the day of the event.

Hot Hors d'Oeuvres

These tempting bites—hot out of the oven—are always impressive. Much of their preparation can be done ahead, too, but they do require last-minute timing. For this reason, I recommend adding only one or two hot items to menus for large parties, and carefully planning your tasks ahead for smaller dinner parties so you have enough time to attend to all your dishes. Delicious hot choices include bruschetta with one of four zesty toppings (pages 125–27), Chicken Skewers with Peanut Dipping Sauce (page 99), or Bacon & Onion Tartlets (page 107).

Understanding Hors d'Oeuvre Ingredients

Some of the most well-known ingredients associated with hors d'oeuvres include luxury items such as cured salmon, caviar, and oysters. But there are countless everyday ingredients that can be transformed into delicious hors d'oeuvres, too. Avocados mashed into guacamole, olives chopped into tapenade, and spinach mixed with feta cheese and folded into filo triangles are all festive foods. Seek out the freshest, highest-quality ingredients for the best results.

Dip & Spread Ingredients

Dried beans, which provide a neutral base for bold spices and fresh herbs, form the base for many dips. Cooked from scratch, they have a wonderful texture and taste. Buy them from markets with a high rate of product turnover to avoid old beans, which take longer to rehydrate and cook.

For the best salsa, use ripe tomatoes, plump limes, and firm chiles and onions. When making Guacamole (page 60), buy dark, pebbly-skinned Hass avocados (other types are generally inferior) several

days ahead to ensure that you have ripe ones to use.

Shop for Kalamata or Niçoise olives, both of them black and brine-cured, for Tapenade (page 63). Anchovies add depth and saltiness without tasting "fishy." Rinsing them briefly and patting them dry will tame their flavor a little.

Earthy dried porcini, sold in bulk or small packages, and fresh shiitake mushrooms flavor Mushroom Pâté (page 64). When using fresh shiitakes, make sure they have firm, dry unbroken

caps, and twist out and discard the entire stem, which is typically quite tough.

Cold Hors d'Oeuvre Ingredients

Cheeses, from delicate cream cheese and fresh goat cheese to more assertive Gorgonzola and Roquefort, star in cold hors d'oeuvres. They can be spread on toasts or crackers or used as a base for fillings. Specialty items like caviar and smoked salmon are usually used in small quantities but add a great deal of flavor. Sour cream or crème fraîche and

mayonnaise are often used for binding the mixtures for filling mushrooms, cherry tomatoes, endive leaves, or small potatoes. Ask for paper-thin slices of prosciutto so you can easily wrap them around chunks of melon or fresh figs.

When making seafood hors d'oeuvres, buy the freshest fish, shrimp (prawns), or shellfish you can find—preferably on the day you plan to serve them—and always keep them refrigerated. You'll want the most pristine pieces of fresh tuna or salmon when making tartare, and a whole salmon fillet for Gravlax (page 87). Oysters, too, must be absolutely fresh. Buy all your seafood from a top-quality seafood merchant.

Hot Hors d'Oeuvre Ingredients

Shop for the best meat, chicken, shrimp, and vegetables for making skewers.

Perishable ingredients, such as live clams, should be kept as cold as possible. To keep clams in the refrigerator for several hours, place them in a colander on a tray so they are not standing in water, and cover them loosely with layers of wet paper towels, never plastic. Live shellfish such as clams (or oysters) will die if left in water or sealed in an airtight container.

Fresh large eggs, all-purpose (plain) and cake flours, and unsalted butter are used for baked hors d'oeuvres, such as tartlets or turnovers. Savory fillings for such items start with heavy (double) cream and eggs, and may include pancetta or bacon, shallots, onions, colorful vegetables, and flavorful cheeses. Filo dough is another flaky pastry choice. Plan ahead if you are using frozen filo dough, as it needs a day to thaw in the refrigerator before using.

Herbs, Spices & Other Seasonings

Fresh green herbs add both flavor and color to hors d'oeuvres. Beyond fresh flat-leaf (Italian) parsley and basil, consider cilantro (fresh coriander), mint, and dill. Look for bright green leaves and refrigerate herbs for longer life.

Keep your spices in a cool, dark place and replace them every six months for the best flavor. Grating nutmeg and grinding black peppercorns or other whole spices just before using makes a significant difference in taste.

Other hors d'oeuvre seasoning basics include kosher salt (superior in flavor to table salt), extra-virgin olive oil, Dijon mustard, and an assortment of vinegars, including sherry, balsamic, rice, and red or white wine vinegar. Soy sauce, capers, fresh ginger, garlic, jalapeños, and citrus all add flavor accents, too.

Cooking, Seasoning & Garnishing Hors d'Oeuvres

The recipes in this book include many techniques, from chopping and mixing fresh ingredients for a quick salsa to fitting molds with pastry dough and adding a savory filling. However, there are some basic rules that you can apply to nearly every recipe. These guidelines teach you how to read a recipe in advance, properly measure ingredients, taste and adjust seasonings, and add a simple garnish—all lessons you can use no matter what you are cooking.

Mise en Place

After you've determined your menu, carefully read each recipe from beginning to end and assemble your *mise en place*. This French culinary term translates to "set in place," and it calls for organizing all the ingredients and equipment you will need for each dish before you start to cook. This includes measuring, chopping, and preparing ingredients and having your pots, pans, knives, and other tools at the ready.

For long-cooking recipes, you may be able to spread out your *mise en place*, preparing the next ingredient while the first one is cooking. I have developed the master recipes in this book to help you set up your *mise en place* as you go— teaching you a valuable routine you can use whenever you cook.

A Guide to Measuring

Correctly measuring your ingredients helps ensure the best results, especially for beginning cooks. Measure liquids in clear glass or plastic measuring cups.

These cups have spouts and markings on the sides indicating fractions of a cup and fluid ounces. Use metal or sturdy plastic, flat-top cups for measuring dry ingredients, spooning them in and then sweeping off the excess with the dull edge of a knife to level the ingredients with the rim. Use the same measuring spoons for both wet and dry ingredients. Look for a set with bowls narrow enough to slip into spice jars. Again, level off dry ingredients with the dull edge of a knife.

Read a recipe's ingredients list carefully, noting whether it says to measure an ingredient before or after it has been chopped. This is especially critical for fresh herbs, where the amounts can vary dramatically.

Seasoning Hors d'Oeuvres

Tasting your recipes along the way and learning to adjust the seasonings are the hallmarks of any good cook. Sometimes all it takes to make a dish taste better is a pinch more of salt, another grind of pepper, or a couple drops of fresh lemon juice. As you make the recipes in this book, one of the most important lessons you will learn is to trust your instincts and adjust the seasonings in each dish as you cook and then again just before serving. Once you have practiced the guidelines I have set out in each recipe, you will have a good idea of the flavor balances you like. Soon you will be able to judge for yourself when a recipe needs

Developing Your Seasoning Palate

Salt is the most basic flavor enhancer for savory cooking, followed closely by freshly ground pepper and fresh lemon juice. Always keep these seasonings ready when you are cooking. Remember to use them in small amounts at first, then taste and adjust if needed.

If your recipe contains raw eggs, be careful not to taste it until after the eggs are cooked.

more fresh herbs to heighten its flavors, or a sprinkle of cayenne or drop of hot-pepper sauce to brighten its overall taste. Part of learning to cook is establishing your own preferences and then applying them as you like.

It is also important to remember that each time you cook, even if you are preparing a recipe you have made before, you may need to make some adjustments. Fresh herbs bought in the beginning of summer often taste different from those you find at the end of the season, so you may want to add a little more or less. Also, keep in mind that many hors d'oeuvres, such as White Bean Dip (page 51), Gravlax (page 87), and Tapenade (page 63), need time to mellow to develop their full flavor. You'll need to take this into account to make sure you set aside enough time to prepare them.

Garnishes for Hors d'Oeuvres

A simple garnish elevates the appearance of almost any hors d'oeuvre. A traditional topping of chopped fresh parsley or green (spring) onions is quick and easy and can be sprinkled lightly or generously as you see fit. You can also carefully place delicate dill fronds, a cross of fresh chives, or small herb sprigs onto individual hors d'oeuvres for a more refined finish. Chopped toasted nuts, which add both texture and flavor, are an excellent garnish, too.

Sprinkle sesame seeds or dust paprika or a different spice used in the recipe over the finished hors d'oeuvres for another last-minute touch. Remember, too, all the garnishes you use should be edible. If you are in doubt about what to pick, choose an ingredient that repeats a flavor used in the dish.

Kitchen Safety

Keeping a clean kitchen is the basis for good and safe cooking. Use lots of hot, soapy water to scrub down your work surfaces after each use, especially after handling raw meat, poultry, or seafood. In fact, it's best to reserve one cutting board for meats and another for fresh produce.

Do not allow hors d'oeuvres that contain meat, fish, poultry, seafood, eggs, or mayonnaise (which are susceptible to bacteria) to remain in the "danger zone," anything warmer than 40°F (4°C), for longer than 2 hours. On a very warm day, reduce this time to 1 hour.

Serving Hors d'Oeuvres

Planning is the key to successful entertaining. Once you have decided on the style of your party and how many people will be attending, you must select your menu, shop efficiently, organize your cooking space, pick out attractive platters and bowls for serving, and set aside enough time to prepare your recipes without rushing. Finally, as you confidently offer the finished hors d'oeuvres to your guests, savor the compliments and enjoy your hard work.

Serving Styles

What kind of party do you want to give? Will it be a casual get-together in your backyard, a buffet-style cocktail party for a large crowd, or perhaps an appetizer or two served with a glass of wine and then a sit-down dinner? This is the first decision you need to make.

For casual gatherings, consider attractive bowls of dips and spreads with a variety of accompaniments, including crudités such as carrot, celery, and bell pepper (capsicum) sticks (pages 34–35) and homemade Tortilla Chips (page 24) or Potato Chips (page 26).

If you are planning a large event, a buffet may be the best solution. Platters of Chicken Skewers with Peanut Dipping Sauce (page 99), Stuffed Vegetables with Herbed Cheese Filling (page 69) or other stuffings (pages 74–75), or an elegant terrine of Mushroom Pâté (page 64) surrounded by Toasts (page 22) are all selections perfect for letting guests help themselves. Passing hors d'oeuvres on trays is a little more formal but works especially well for serving hot items.

Often, the best way to serve hors d'oeuvres at parties is to combine a variety of serving styles. Set up a drink bar on one side of the room and offer a few buffet-type stations with dips and spreads throughout the area so guests can easily mingle. In addition, offer a few passed cold or hot items—this will help you circulate among your guests.

Hors d'oeuvres don't need to be limited to large gatherings, however. Try Tapenade (page 63) or Bruschetta with Olives & Roasted Peppers (page 125) as a prelude to a dinner party, rather than the more expected first course of soup or salad.

Planning the Menu

When putting together a menu of hors d'oeuvres, it is important to consider the serving temperatures of your selections. Hot hors d'oeuvres will need last-minute cooking and plating. Although some of them will still taste delicious at room temperature, they will take you away from your guests while you prepare to serve them. Cold hors d'oeuvres, dips, and spreads are easier to make ahead and can be kept ready to serve. For large events, select a few of each type for a well-rounded menu.

Your hors d'oeuvres selections should also complement one another. Vary flavors, colors, shapes, textures, and cooking techniques. If you are not sure of your guests' tastes, choose a few mild-flavored appetizers, such as Stuffed Vegetables with Herbed Cheese Filling (page 69) or Deviled Eggs (page 91). If you are serving the hors d'oeuvres before a dinner party, avoid ingredients that duplicate those used in the main course.

You may also want to use your hors d'oeuvres to establish a theme. Guacamole (page 60) is a natural choice before a Southwest barbecue, while Broiled Stuffed Clams (page 128) would be the perfect beginning for a festive New Orleans–style jambalaya party.

Serving Quantities

How many hors d'oeuvres should you serve? The answer depends entirely on the event. If your hors d'oeuvres are preceding a dinner, 4 or 5 bites per person are sufficient to whet the appetite of your guests—not suppress it. An after-work or cocktails-only get-together requires generous amounts of hors d'oeuvres, typically 8–10 bites per person for every 1 to 1½ hours. For an average-

Making Lists

A guest list, menu, and a shopping list may be the first lists you make when planning a party, but there are other helpful lists you can make, too.

Don't forget to make a list of what you are serving and when you are serving it for quick reference and timing. Note if cold hors d'oeuvres need to be taken out of the refrigerator at a certain time. For hot items, write down oven temperature, length of baking or broiling time, and set a timer. Remember, you may need to have your oven preheated for the first hot hors d'oeuvres before your guests arrive.

sized party of 8–20 guests at which only appetizers will be served, plan on serving 5 or 6 different hors d'oeuvres (2 hot and 2 cold items that can be passed and 1 or 2 buffet items). If you are hosting a larger event with 30–40 guests, add another hot hors d'oeuvre to each category.

Timing & Planning Ahead

Timing is a critical element to successful entertaining. Do as much as you can to prepare for any party in advance. This includes shopping for ingredients, preparing your vegetables and pastry doughs, and checking your serving dishes to determine what you may need.

The recipes in this book often include extra tips for planning ahead. When reading through them, note when dips, spreads, pastry doughs, and fillings can or should be made ahead.

Finally, don't wait until the day of the party to clean house, arrange furniture, or wash wineglasses. Instead, spend the minutes before your guests arrive adding thoughtful finishing touches.

Presenting Hors d'Oeuvres

Gathering an assortment of attractive serving pieces for presenting your hors d'oeuvres is a good investment for entertaining. Keep an eye out for interesting baskets and different sizes of serving plates and platters. A selection of cloth napkins is handy for lining glass or metal bowls or baskets.

When deciding on serving dishes, keep size in mind. If the appetizers are very small, for example, place them on a small plate. Don't forget to provide knives or spoons if you are serving spreads. When arranging hors d'oeuvres, position them

on the platter so that one bite can be removed without touching the others. Cold hors d'oeuvres are best served on cool or chilled plates, and hot hors d'oeuvres should be placed on warmed plates. To warm plates and/or platters, place them in a 200°F (95°C) oven for about 15 minutes.

If your group is large, use two small bowls instead of one large container, and place them in two different locations. Keep a watchful eye and remove nearly empty serving plates and refill them in the kitchen, or replace them with a fresh plate you've already prepared. Quietly remove napkins, plates, and glasses that accumulate on tables.

Once you have mastered these tips and practiced making some of the recipes in the pages ahead, you will be ready to plan, prepare, and enjoy many hors d'oeuvres.

1

Basic Recipes

The best hors d'oeuvres begin with a solid foundation, and the recipes in this chapter are designed to give you just that. Here you'll find two foolproof recipes for pastry doughs that can be used for tender, flaky tartlets and turnovers. And once you've made pita crisps, toasts, toast cups, tortilla chips, and potato chips from scratch, you'll never want to use store-bought accompaniments again.

½ cup (4 oz/125 g) cold unsalted butter

1 cold large egg

1 cup (5 oz/155 g) unbleached all-purpose (plain) flour

¼ cup (1 oz/30 g) cake (soft-wheat) flour

½ teaspoon kosher salt

MAKES ENOUGH DOUGH FOR SIXTEEN 4½-INCH (11.5-CM) FLUTED BARQUETTE MOLDS OR 2½–2¾-INCH (6–7-CM) PLAIN OR FLUTED ROUND TARTLET PANS

Tartlet Dough

Some pastry doughs are fragile and can be difficult to work with, but the addition of an egg firms up this dough, making it easy to mix and to roll out thinly and evenly. The use of cake flour, which is low in gluten (the elastic protein in wheat), helps give the dough a tender texture.

1 Cut the butter into pieces and beat the egg

Using a chef's knife or a bench scraper, cut the butter into 1-inch (2.5-cm) pieces. Break the egg into a small bowl and, using a fork, stir until the yolk and white are completely blended. Both the butter and egg must be cold from the refrigerator so the butter will remain in distinct flakes, rather than be absorbed by the flour. Otherwise, the pastry will be tough, rather than flaky and crisp.

2 Mix the dry ingredients

Fit a food processor with the metal blade. Put the unbleached flour, cake flour, and salt in the food processor. Pulse the machine just until the ingredients are well mixed. (Alternatively, make the dough by hand: Put the unbleached flour, cake flour, and salt in a mixing bowl and stir with a rubber spatula until the ingredients are well mixed.)

3 Mix in the butter

Add the butter pieces to the work bowl and process with on-off pulses until the butter has flattened into flakes and the rest of the mixture looks like grated Parmesan cheese, about 5 seconds. Some butter particles will remain larger than others. When these larger pieces melt in the heat of the oven, the liquid evaporates, creating empty pockets in the dough that make the pastry flaky. (If you are making the dough by hand, scatter the butter pieces over the flour mixture in the bowl. Using the fingers of 1 hand, pinch the butter and flour between your thumb and fingertips until the butter has flattened into flakes and the rest of the mixture looks like grated Parmesan cheese.)

Mix in the egg

4 Using a rubber spatula, scrape down the sides of the work bowl to bring all of the ingredients together. Turn on the processor and, with the motor running, quickly pour the blended egg through the feed tube and process with on-off pulses just until the mixture comes together in clumps; do not allow it to form a ball. If you process the dough beyond this point, it will toughen. (If you are making the dough by hand, pour the blended egg over the mixture in the bowl and mix it in, using 1 hand to squeeze the dough until it just comes together in clumps; do not overwork the dough.)

Shape the dough

5 Turn the dough out onto a lightly floured work surface. Using both hands, gently push the dough into a single mass. Work quickly so that the dough remains cold. You do not want the butter to begin to melt. Using your hands and a bench scraper, shape the dough into a flat rectangle about 6 by 3½ inches (15 by 9 cm).

Let the dough rest

6 Place the dough in a locking plastic bag or wrap well in plastic wrap and refrigerate it for at least 2 hours. This rest period relaxes the gluten—the elastic protein in the flour—so the dough will be easier to roll out. It also allows the moisture to permeate the dough thoroughly, creating an even texture. (At this point, you can also refrigerate the dough for up to 2 days or freeze it for up to 1 month before rolling it out. If you are freezing the dough, let it thaw in the refrigerator overnight before using.)

CHEF'S TIP

If you tend to have warm hands, rinse them under running cold water and dry them well before handling the dough. This will keep your hands from causing the dough to soften too much.

Turnover Dough

Sour cream gives this pastry a rich flavor and melt-in-your-mouth texture. But it also results in a softer dough than one made with egg. This means that once you start working with the dough, it may need a few resting periods in the refrigerator along the way to ensure successful rolling and shaping.

½ cup (4 oz/125 g) cold unsalted butter

1 cup (5 oz/155 g) unbleached all-purpose (plain) flour

¼ cup (1 oz/30 g) cake (soft-wheat) flour

½ teaspoon kosher salt

¼ cup (2 oz/60 g) cold sour cream

MAKES ENOUGH DOUGH FOR 24–28 TURNOVERS, EACH 3 INCHES (7.5 CM) LONG

1 **Cut the butter into pieces**
Using a chef's knife or a bench scraper, cut the butter into 1-inch (2.5-cm) pieces. The butter must be cold from the refrigerator so it will remain in distinct flakes, rather than be absorbed by the flour. Otherwise, the pastry will be tough, rather than flaky and crisp.

2 **Mix the dry ingredients**
Fit a food processor with the metal blade. Put the unbleached flour, cake flour, and salt in the food processor. Pulse the machine just until the ingredients are well mixed. (Alternatively, make the dough by hand: Put the unbleached flour, cake flour, and salt in a mixing bowl and stir with a rubber spatula until the ingredients are well mixed.)

3 **Mix in the butter and add the sour cream**
Add the butter pieces to the work bowl and process with on-off pulses until the butter has flattened into flakes and the rest of the mixture looks like grated Parmesan cheese, about 5 seconds. Some butter particles will remain larger than others. When these larger pieces melt in the heat of the oven, the liquid evaporates, creating empty pockets in the dough that make the pastry flaky. Using a rubber spatula, scrape down the sides of the work bowl to bring all the ingredients together. Spoon the sour cream over the other ingredients in the processor. The sour cream must be cold, too, so that the butter stays cold and remains in distinct flakes. (If you are making the dough by hand, scatter the butter pieces over the flour mixture in the bowl. Using the fingers of 1 hand, pinch the butter and flour between your thumb and fingertips until the butter has flattened into flakes and the rest of the mixture looks like grated Parmesan cheese. Add the sour cream.)

   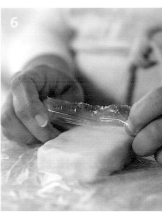

4 Gently process the dough
Turn the processor on and process with on-off pulses just until the mixture comes together in clumps; do not allow it to form a ball. If you process the dough beyond this point, it will toughen. (If you are making the dough by hand, mix in the sour cream, using 1 hand to squeeze the dough until it just comes together in clumps; do not overwork the dough.)

5 Shape the dough
Turn the dough out onto a lightly floured work surface. Using both hands, gently push the dough into a single mass. Work quickly so that the dough remains cool. You do not want the butter to begin to melt. Using your hands and a bench scraper, divide the dough in half. Shape each half into a flat rectangle about 3½ by 2½ inches (9 by 6 cm).

6 Let the dough rest
Place the dough rectangles in separate locking plastic bags or wrap well in plastic wrap and refrigerate them for at least 2 hours. This rest period relaxes the gluten—the elastic protein in the flour—so the dough will be easier to roll out. It also allows the moisture to permeate the dough thoroughly, creating an even texture. (At this point, you can also refrigerate the dough for up to 2 days or freeze it for up to 1 month before rolling it out. If you are freezing the dough, let it thaw in the refrigerator overnight before using.)

CHEF'S TIP
When working with pastry dough, it is helpful to use cold equipment along with cold ingredients. A marble surface is ideal for rolling out the dough. It stays cool, so the pastry has less chance of warming up and becoming too soft.

Canapé Bases

These crisps, toasts, and cups are used either as sturdy trenchers for holding spreads, pâtés, and the like or as scoops for dunking into salsas and dips. Follow steps 1 and 2 for pita crisps, 3 and 4 for toasts, or 5 and 6 for toast cups. Step 7 explains how to keep each one crisp until serving.

For pita crisps

3 pita bread rounds

1–2 tablespoons extra-virgin olive oil

Paprika for dusting

Poppy seeds, sesame seeds, or fennel seeds for sprinkling, optional

MAKES 72 PITA CRISPS

For toasts

1 sweet baguette

3–4 tablespoons extra-virgin olive oil, optional

MAKES 24–36 TOASTS

For toast cups

2 tablespoons unsalted butter, melted

24 thin slices white bread

MAKES 24 TOAST CUPS

1 **Preheat the oven and slice the pita bread rounds**
Preheat the oven to 325°F (165°C). Stack the pita bread rounds. Using a serrated knife, cut the stack in half. Then cut each half in half again, so the pitas are quartered. Finally, cut each stacked quarter into thirds, to create 12 triangles from each pita (36 triangles total). Starting at the point of each triangle, carefully open it until it lies flat and slice through the seam to separate the 2 layers, to create 24 triangles from each pita, or 72 triangles total.

2 **Make the pita crisps**
Arrange the triangles in a single layer and close together on rimmed baking sheets. Brush each triangle lightly with some of the olive oil, then dust with paprika. Sprinkle with seeds, if desired. (Use the seeds if they complement the flavors in the hors d'oeuvres the crisps will accompany. For example, fennel seeds are a good choice for sprinkling on pita crisps served with Salmon Tartare with Fennel & Lemon on page 85 because the tartare contains fresh fennel. Consider sesame seeds for sprinkling on pita crisps served with White Bean Dip on page 51. The nutty flavor of the seeds pairs well with the fresh herbs and lemon juice in the dip.) Bake the triangles until they are dry, crisp, and golden brown, 10–15 minutes. Let cool completely on the baking sheets.

3 **Preheat the oven and cut the baguette**
Preheat the oven to 300°F (150°C). Using a serrated knife, cut the baguette on the diagonal into 24–36 slices, each about ¼ inch (6 mm) thick. Save any remaining baguette for another use, or cut more slices if you are planning to use the toasts to accompany more than one recipe.

4 Make the toasts

Arrange the baguette slices in a single layer on rimmed baking sheets and brush them lightly with the olive oil, if using. (The olive oil will add flavor and color. Brushing it on bread to be toasted for hors d'oeuvres is a common practice in Italy, where the toasts are called *crostini*. If you are serving the toasts with an Italian-inspired bean dip such as the Cannellini Bean & Roasted Red Pepper Dip on page 57, the oil is a traditional addition.) Bake the slices, turning once, until dried, crisp, and tinged with gold, about 45 minutes. (Alternatively, preheat the broiler/grill. Arrange the bread slices in a single layer on rimmed baking sheets and brush them lightly with the olive oil, if using. Broil/grill, turning once, until dried, crisp, and tinged with gold, 3–4 minutes. If you use the broiler, watch the toasts carefully, as they can burn easily.) Let the toasts cool completely on the baking sheets.

5 Preheat the oven, prepare the pan, and cut the bread

Preheat the oven to 400°F (200°C). Brush the inside of 24 miniature muffin cups with the melted butter. Using a rolling pin, roll the bread on a work surface until it is as thin as possible. Using a 3-inch (7.5-cm) round plain or fluted pastry cutter, cut out a round from each slice.

6 Make the toast cups

One at a time, fit a bread round into each prepared muffin cup, gently pushing it down into the bottom and up the sides. Bake until golden brown, about 10 minutes. Use tongs to remove the toast cups gently from the pans and transfer to wire racks to cool.

7 Store the pita crisps, toasts, or toast cups

The pita crisps, toasts, and toast cups all taste best when eaten within 2 hours of being made. However, if you need to make them in advance, you can keep them overnight in an airtight container.

CHEF'S TIP

Technically, canapé bases are made from small pieces of bread or a similar grain-based item. However, rounds of a crisp vegetable such as cucumber can be a refreshing alternative. To make fluted cucumber canapé bases, see page 41.

Tortilla Chips

A properly cooked tortilla chip hot out of the oil is light, crisp, and golden brown, and never greasy. Seek out a superfine salt for the best results when seasoning. It clings more easily to the chips than regular table salt, resulting in a more satisfying flavor and texture.

8 small corn tortillas, each 6–6½ inches (15–16.5 cm) in diameter

About 8 cups (64 fl oz/2 l) corn oil or peanut oil for deep-frying

Fine sea salt for sprinkling

MAKES 4–6 SERVINGS

CHEF'S TIP
Popcorn salt, a superfine salt, is a great option for seasoning homemade tortilla and potato chips because it clings so well to a fried surface. It can be found in many supermarkets or can easily be purchased online.

1 Cut the tortillas into triangles

Stack the tortillas. Using a serrated knife, cut the stack in half. Then cut each half in half again, so the tortillas are quartered. Finally, cut each stacked quarter in half again, to create 8 triangles from each tortilla (64 triangles total). Arrange the triangles in a single layer on rimmed baking sheets. If time allows, let the tortilla pieces dry on the baking sheets at room temperature for several hours or up to overnight. If you want the tortillas to stay flat while frying, cover them with another baking sheet while they are drying, and weight the top sheet with heavy cans.

2 Prepare to fry the tortilla triangles

A wok 12–14 inches (30–35 cm) in diameter, with its rounded bottom and gradually sloping sides, is ideal for deep-frying on a gas stove. It provides the maximum surface with the least amount of oil. A flat-bottomed wok works well for an electric stove. If you don't have a wok, use a large, deep heavy pot. If the sizes of your gas burners vary, place the wok ring on the largest burner on your stove, then rest the wok in it (the wok for the electric stove sits directly on the burner). Pour in the oil to a depth of about 2 inches (5 cm). The pan should never be more than half full, or the oil could spatter dangerously when it bubbles up. Line 1 or 2 large rimmed baking sheets with several layers of paper towels for draining the fried chips and place them near the stove. Have ready a skimmer for turning and retrieving the tortilla chips.

3 **Fry the first batch of tortilla triangles**
Turn on your kitchen ventilation and attach a deep-frying thermometer to your wok or pot. Turn on the burner to medium-high heat and heat the oil to 375°F (190°C) on the thermometer. This may take up to 10 minutes, depending on your stove. Don't walk away—you don't want the oil to get too hot. Carefully drop enough tortilla triangles into the oil to form a single layer on the surface (up to half of the triangles). If you add more, the temperature of the oil will drop and the triangles will absorb the oil, resulting in greasy chips. If you are concerned about oil spatters, use the skimmer to ease the tortilla triangles into the oil. Fry the triangles, using the skimmer to turn them frequently, until they are crisp and medium-brown, 2–3 minutes. Don't let them get too dark, or they will taste bitter.

4 **Drain the tortilla chips**
Using the skimmer, lift the tortilla chips out of the oil and place on the paper towel–lined baking sheets. (It's okay if some of the chips overlap.) Blot the tops of the chips gently with additional paper towels.

5 **Fry the remaining tortilla triangles**
Allow the oil temperature to return to 375°F. Repeat the frying and draining steps with the remaining tortilla triangles, letting the oil heat to 375°F before frying each batch.

6 **Season the chips and serve or store**
Lightly sprinkle the chips with salt. To serve, transfer the chips to a bowl or napkin-lined basket.

CHEF'S TIP
If you don't have a deep-frying thermometer, use a plain wooden chopstick to gauge the temperature of the oil. When you think the oil is hot enough for frying, immerse the end of the chopstick in the oil. The oil is ready if it immediately bubbles up around the chopstick.

Potato Chips

Paper-thin and golden brown, these homemade chips have a far superior taste than their store-bought cousins. Whether you use russets or Yukon golds, the chips boast a full flavor heightened by a sprinkling of salt. Frying them twice ensures that the potatoes cook through and that the chips will be extra crisp.

6 large russet potatoes or Yukon gold potatoes, 1¾–2 lb (875 g–1 kg) total weight

About 8 cups (64 fl oz/2 l) corn oil or peanut oil for deep-frying

Fine sea salt for sprinkling

MAKES 4–6 SERVINGS

CHEF'S TIP
For rustic-looking (and rustic-tasting) potato chips, leave the peels on. Just be sure to scrub the potatoes well with a vegetable brush under running cold water before slicing.

1 **Peel and slice the potatoes**
Using a vegetable peeler, peel the potatoes and transfer them to a large bowl of cool water. Potatoes quickly turn brown when exposed to air; the water prevents discoloration. One by one, remove the potatoes from the water and, using a chef's knife, mandoline, or mandoline-style kitchen slicer, slice the potatoes into rounds ¹⁄₁₆ inch (2 mm) thick, or as thin as possible. Return the slices to the water.

2 **Prepare to fry the potato slices**
A wok 12–14 inches (30–35 cm) in diameter, with its rounded bottom and gradually sloping sides, is ideal for deep-frying on a gas stove. It provides the maximum surface with the least amount of oil. A flat-bottomed wok works well for an electric stove. If you don't have a wok, use a large, deep heavy pot. If the sizes of your gas burners vary, place the wok ring on the largest burner on your stove, then rest the wok in it (the wok for the electric stove sits directly on the burner). Pour in the oil to a depth of about 2 inches (5 cm). The pan should never be more than half full, or the oil could spatter dangerously when it bubbles up. Attach a deep-frying thermometer to your wok or pot. Line 4 rimmed baking sheets with paper towels to hold the potatoes in a single layer after they are dried. Have ready a skimmer for turning and retrieving the potato chips.

3 **Drain and thoroughly dry the potatoes**
Drain the potato slices, spin them dry in a salad spinner, and then spread them out onto the paper towel–lined baking sheets. Pat dry with additional paper towels. Drying the potato slices thoroughly will help them brown evenly and keep the oil from spattering while they are frying.

4 Fry the potato slices the first time

Turn on your kitchen ventilation. Turn on the burner to medium-high heat and heat the oil to 325°F (165°C) on the thermometer. This may take up to 10 minutes, depending on your stove. Don't walk away—you don't want the oil to get too hot. Put about 1 cup (4 oz/125 g) of the dried potato slices into a bowl. Standing back, carefully turn the bowl over to slip the slices into the hot oil. If you add more, the temperature of the oil will drop and the slices will absorb the oil, resulting in greasy chips. Fry the potatoes, using the skimmer to turn them occasionally, until they look firm and start to crisp around the edges, about 3 minutes. While the potatoes are frying, line the baking sheets with clean paper towels. Using the skimmer, lift the potato slices out of the oil and place in a single layer on the lined baking sheets. Allow the oil temperature to return to 325°F before frying and draining the remaining potato slices in the same way.

5 Let the potato slices cool

Let the potato slices cool for at least 15 minutes or up to 6 hours. Their exterior surface will cool down immediately while their interior will continue to cook. This cooling period guarantees the potatoes will be cooked through and ready to be browned and crisped when they return to the wok for a second frying.

6 Fry the potato slices a second time

Line 2 of the baking sheets with clean paper towels. Reheat the oil over medium-high heat to 375°F (190°C). Again working in 1-cup batches, slip the potato slices into the oil. Cook the potatoes, turning them continuously with the skimmer, until they are crisp and medium brown; this will take only 1–2 minutes. Don't let them get too dark, or they will taste bitter. Using the skimmer, transfer the potatoes to the clean paper towels. (It's okay if some of the chips overlap.) Blot the tops with additional paper towels. Allow the oil to reheat to 375°F. Repeat to fry and drain the remaining slices, letting the oil heat to 375°F before frying each batch.

7 Season the chips and serve or store

Lightly sprinkle the chips with salt. To serve, transfer the chips to a bowl or a napkin-lined basket.

CHEF'S TIP

You can save the oil from deep-frying and re-use it once or twice. To recycle the oil, first make sure that it has cooled completely. Then set a funnel in the mouth of an empty bottle or jar and ladle the oil through the funnel. Cover the bottle or jar and store in a cool, dark place. Discard if the oil darkens or develops an off odor.

2

Key Techniques

Mastering the following key culinary techniques will make preparing hors d'oeuvres—and many other recipes—much easier. In the pages ahead, you will learn some specific skills, such as how to use a pastry bag to pipe rosettes of filling or how to shuck a raw oyster. You will also learn some invaluable everyday techniques, including how to quickly dice an onion or roast a bell pepper (capsicum).

Using a Pastry Bag

1 Insert the tip
Insert a pastry tip inside the hole at the narrow end of a 12-inch (30-cm) or larger pastry bag. Push the tip firmly into the narrow opening so that it extends beyond the hole.

2 Twist to close the bag
Twist the pastry bag directly above the tip and push the bag into the tip. This ensures that nothing will leak out while you fill the bag.

3 Form a cuff
Turn down about 2 inches (5 cm) at the top end of the bag to form a cuff. The cuff makes the bag easier to fill and keeps any piping mixture from getting on the outside of the bag.

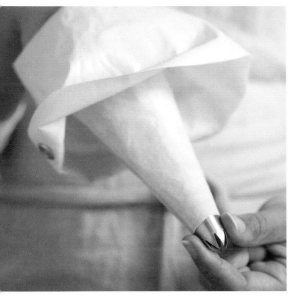

5 Unroll the cuff and release the tip
Unroll the cuff and gather the ends of the bag in one hand. Pull the tip and untwist it to allow the filling to flow into the tip.

6 Ease the filling into the tip
Starting at the top end of the bag, gently squeeze the contents until the filling reaches the tip.

7 Prepare to pipe
Twist and hold the top of the bag with one hand; this hand controls the rate of flow. Guide the tip with the index finger and thumb of the other hand.

4 Fill the bag

Using a rubber spatula, transfer the piping mixture into the bag, filling it no more than two-thirds full.

Rolling Out Pastry Dough

1 Prepare to roll the dough

Place the dough between 2 long sheets of waxed paper. Give the dough several whacks with a rolling pin to flatten and soften it a bit. This gives you a good start.

2 Roll out the dough

Starting with the pin ¼ inch (6 mm) from one edge, begin rolling, pushing outward smoothly and stopping ¼ inch from the other edge (so the edges don't get too thin).

8 Pipe the filling

Hold the tip where you would like to pipe. Apply gentle pressure to pipe a rosette. When the rosette is complete, release the pressure, twirl the bag to break off the tip, and lift the bag away.

3 Lift, rotate, and flip the dough

Lift the dough, rotate it a quarter turn, and repeat rolling, again starting at the edge. Flip the dough over from time to time to ensure that it rolls out evenly.

TROUBLESHOOTING

When rolling out pastry dough, be sure to straighten the waxed paper if it develops wrinkles. This way your dough will be perfectly smooth and have an even thickness.

Trimming Asparagus

1 Bend the spears

The best way to trim fresh asparagus is to bend the cut end of each spear until it breaks naturally. The spear will snap precisely where the fibrous, tough inedible portion begins.

Trimming Green or Yellow Beans

1 Break off the stem ends

Using your fingers, break off the tough stem ends of the beans where they were attached to the plant.

Trimming Broccoli

1 Cut off the leaves and stalks

Using a chef's knife, trim away any remaining leaves on the broccoli stalk, then cut off the bottom portion of the stalk. (You can peel this lower portion and cook it later for another dish.)

2 Trim the ends

Next, line the spears up on your cutting board and trim off the ends to create pieces that are the same length. Asparagus spears should be about 5 inches (13 cm) long for crudités.

2 Remove any strings

Nowadays, most green beans have no "strings." If you do find a wispy string attached to the stem end, pull it along the length of the bean to remove it. Leave the pointed tail ends intact.

2 Cut the broccoli into florets

Using a paring knife, cut the broccoli head into individual florets, each about 1¾ inches (4.5 cm) long. If the stems of the florets seem tough, use the paring knife to peel them.

Trimming Cauliflower

1 Remove the core and leaves

Using a chef's knife, cut the head of cauliflower in half vertically to reveal the core. Use a paring knife to cut out the inner core and trim away any green leaves.

Blanching Vegetables

1 Briefly boil the vegetables

Bring a large pot three-fourths full of water to a boil. When the water is boiling, add about 2 teaspoons kosher salt and the vegetables to be blanched, in this case, asparagus.

2 Remove the blanched vegetables

As soon as the vegetables are crisp and barely tender (taste a piece), remove them with a skimmer or slotted spoon. For smaller vegetables, drain them in a colander.

2 Cut the cauliflower into florets

Cut the cauliflower head into florets, each about 1¾ inches (4.5 cm) long. If the stems of the florets seem tough, use the paring knife to peel them.

3 Shock the vegetables

Immediately transfer the blanched vegetables to a bowl of ice water. This will stop the cooking and set the color, a technique known as *shocking*.

4 Pat the vegetables dry

When cool, once again remove the vegetables from the water or drain them in a colander. Pat them dry with a kitchen towel or paper towels.

Cutting Carrot Sticks

1 Peel and trim the carrots
Start with good-quality, unblemished carrots. Use a vegetable peeler to remove the rough skin. Using a paring knife, trim off the leafy tops and rootlike ends.

2 Cut the carrots into lengths
Cut the carrots crosswise into 2 or 3 uniform lengths. They should be as long as you would like the final sticks to be; 3 inches (7.5 cm) is about right for crudités.

Cutting Celery Sticks

1 Cut the celery into lengths
Cut trimmed celery stalks crosswise into 2 or 3 uniform lengths. They should be as long as you would like the final sticks to be; 3 inches (7.5 cm) is about right for crudités.

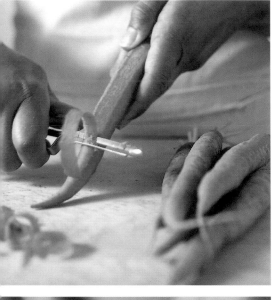

3 Cut the carrots into thirds
Switch to a chef's knife and cut the carrot pieces lengthwise into thirds. Each piece should be about ½ inch (12 mm) wide.

4 Cut the carrots into sticks
Cut each piece lengthwise into sticks. Space your cuts about ½ inch apart.

2 Cut the celery into sticks
Cut the celery pieces lengthwise into sticks. Space your cuts about ½ inch (12 mm) apart.

Cutting Bell Pepper Sticks

1 Halve the bell pepper
Using a chef's knife, cut each bell pepper (capsicum) in half lengthwise. This makes it easier to remove the stem and seeds and will expose the white ribs, or membranes.

2 Remove the stem and seeds
Use your fingers to pull out the stem and most of the seeds. Brush away any lingering seeds and then, using a paring knife, cut away the white ribs.

Pitting Olives

1 Pound the olives
Place the olives in a locking plastic bag, force out the excess air, and seal closed. Using a meat pounder or a rolling pin, gently pound the olives to loosen the pits.

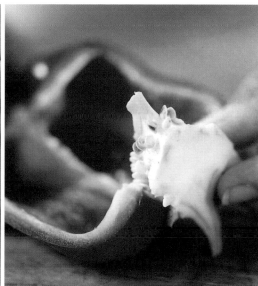

3 Slice off the tops and bottoms
Using the chef's knife, cut a thin slice off the top and bottom of each half. This creates a rectangular length of pepper that can easily be cut into sticks.

4 Cut the halves into sticks
Using your fingers, flatten each pepper half and cut lengthwise to create sticks about ½ inch (12 mm) wide. You should be able to cut about 8 sticks from each half.

2 Remove the pits
Remove the crushed olives from the bag and separate the pits from the olive flesh with your fingers. Use a paring knife to cut the flesh from the pits of any stubborn olives.

Seeding Tomatoes

1 Halve the tomato

To seed round or globe tomatoes, cut them in half through their "equator." Cut plum (Roma) tomatoes in half lengthwise. A sharp chef's knife will work, or use a serrated knife.

Dicing Seeded Tomatoes

1 Cut lengthwise slices

Use a chef's knife to make a shallow circular cut to remove the cores if necessary. Place each half cut side down and make a series of slices, ⅛–¼ inch (3–6 mm) apart.

2 Cut the slices into strips

Stack 2 or 3 of the tomato slices at a time on their sides. Make a second series of slices, ⅛–¼ inch apart, perpendicular to the first. You will end up with strips.

2 Scoop out the seeds

Holding a tomato half over a bowl, use a finger to scoop out the seed sacs and any excess liquid.

3 Cut the strips into dice

Line up the strips and cut across into ⅛- to ¼-inch dice. Push the dice aside to keep it separate from your work area. Repeat steps 1–3 with the remaining tomato halves.

4 Transfer the dice

To remove the diced tomato from the board, use the flat side of the chef's knife to scoop it up and transfer to a glass bowl.

Working with Avocados

1 Halve the avocado lengthwise
Select a ripe avocado; it should yield to gentle finger pressure. Using a chef's knife, cut the avocado in half lengthwise, cutting down to and around the pit.

2 Separate the halves
Hold the avocado so one of the halves rests in each hand. Gently rotate the halves in opposite directions to separate them.

3 Remove the pit
Carefully holding the half with the pit in one hand, strike the pit with the heel of the blade of the chef's knife, lodging it in the pit. Twist the knife and lift out the pit.

4 Score each avocado half
Using a paring knife, score each half by cutting parallel lines just down to the peel. Turn the half 90 degrees and cut another set of parallel lines perpendicular to the first.

5 Release the pieces
Use a large spoon to scoop the avocado pieces into a bowl. Use the avocado pieces as soon as possible after cutting them.

TROUBLESHOOTING
Avocado flesh quickly turns brown when exposed to air. Sprinkling the flesh with a little lemon or lime juice after cutting it into cubes will help slow the discoloration process.

Dicing an Onion or a Shallot

1 Halve the onion or shallot
Using a chef's knife, cut the onion (shown here) or shallot in half lengthwise through the root end. This makes it easier to peel and gives each half a flat side for stability.

2 Peel the onion or shallot
Using a paring knife, pick up the edge of the papery skin at the stem end and pull it away. If the first layer of flesh has rough or papery patches, remove it, too.

3 Trim the onion or shallot
Trim each end neatly, leaving some of the root intact to help hold the onion or shallot half together. Place a half, flat side down and with the root end facing away from you, on the board.

4 Cut the half lengthwise
Hold the half securely on either side. Using a chef's knife, make a series of lengthwise cuts, as thick as you want the final dice to be. Do not cut all the way through the root end.

5 Cut the half horizontally
Spread your fingers across the half to help keep it together. Turn the knife blade parallel to the cutting board and make a series of horizontal cuts as thick as you want the final dice to be.

6 Cut the half crosswise
Still holding the half together with your fingers, cut it crosswise to dice. To mince the pieces, hold the knife tip down with one hand and rock the heel of the knife over them.

Working with Garlic

TECHNIQUE

1 Loosen the garlic peel
Using the flat side of a chef's knife, firmly press against the clove. If you plan to mince the garlic, it's fine to smash it. If you are slicing it, use light pressure to keep the clove intact.

2 Peel and halve the clove
The pressure from the knife will cause the garlic peel to split. Grasp the peel with your fingers and pull off and discard it. Using the chef's knife, cut the garlic clove in half lengthwise.

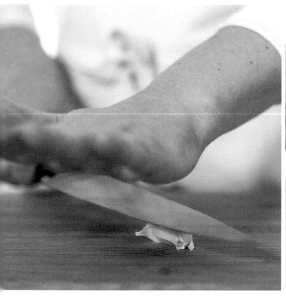

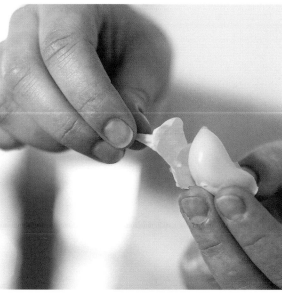

TROUBLESHOOTING
You may see a small green sprout running through the middle of the garlic clove, which, if left in, could impart a bitter flavor to the recipe. Use the tip of a paring knife to pop out the sprout and discard it.

3 Cut the garlic into slices
One at a time, cut the garlic clove halves into very thin slices. Gather the slices in the center of the cutting board to cut into smaller pieces.

4 Chop the garlic
Hold the knife handle with one hand and rest the fingertips of your other hand on the knife tip. Move the knife heel in an up-and-down motion over the garlic until evenly chopped.

5 Mince the garlic
Gather the chopped garlic in a compact pile on the board. Clean the garlic bits off the knife and add them to the pile. Continue to chop until the garlic pieces are very fine, or *minced*.

Working with Leeks

1 Trim the leeks

Using a chef's knife, trim off the roots and dark green tops of the leeks, leaving only the white and pale green parts. If the outer layer is wilted or discolored, peel it away and discard.

2 Halve and quarter the leeks

Cut each leek in half lengthwise. Place each half, cut side down, and halve it again to create quarters.

Working with Green Onions

1 Trim the onions

Using a chef's knife, trim off the roots and tough green tops of the green (spring) onions.

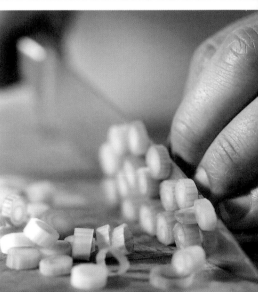

3 Rinse the leeks

Separating the layers with your fingers to expose any sand or dirt, swish the leeks in a bowl of water. You can also rinse the leeks under running water while separating the layers.

4 Slice the leeks crosswise

Holding the layers of each quarter together, pat the leeks dry with a kitchen towel. Using a chef's knife, cut the leek quarters crosswise into slices.

2 Slice the onions crosswise

If the recipe calls for thinly sliced green onions, line up the trimmed ends and slice the onions crosswise. To mince the onions, rock the heel of the knife over the slices.

Peeling & Finely Dicing a Cucumber

1 Peel and halve the cucumber
Use a vegetable peeler to peel away the dark skin from the cucumber (many cucumbers are coated with wax). Using a chef's knife, slice the cucumber in half lengthwise.

2 Scoop out the seeds
Using a small spoon or melon baller, scoop out any seeds and pulpy matter, which can be quite watery. English (hothouse) cucumbers may have few or no seeds.

Making Fluted Cucumber Slices

1 Peel away the skin in stripes
Use a bar-style lemon stripper or vegetable peeler to create stripes of dark green peel and light green flesh.

3 Cut the seeded halves into strips
Cut the cucumber halves lengthwise into slices about ⅛ inch (3 mm) thick. Then, cut each slice lengthwise to create strips ⅛ inch wide.

4 Cut the strips into dice
Line up the strips and cut them at ⅛-inch intervals to dice the cucumber finely. Be sure to keep the tips of your fingers tucked under and away from the knife.

2 Cut the cucumber into slices
Using a chef's knife, cut the cucumber crosswise on the diagonal to create slices ¼ inch (6 mm) thick.

TECHNIQUE

TECHNIQUE

Chopping & Mincing Herbs

1 Separate the leaves

After rinsing and patting dry the herbs, use your fingers to pluck the leaves from the sprigs and discard the stems. Gather the leaves together into a pile on a cutting board.

2 Chop the herb

Rest your fingertips on the tip of a chef's knife and rock the knife over the board to chop the leaves. If the recipe calls for a coarsely chopped herb, chop them briefly.

Toasting Nuts or Seeds

1 Toast the nuts or seeds in a pan

Place the nuts or seeds in a dry frying pan over medium heat. Stir them frequently to keep them from burning.

3 Mince the herb

If the recipe calls for a minced herb, regather the leaves into a compact pile, cleaning the herbs off the knife and adding them to the pile, and continue to chop into very fine pieces.

4 Transfer the leaves

To remove chopped or minced leaves from the board, use the flat side of the knife to scoop them up. Then run your finger carefully along the flat side of the blade to slide them into a dish.

2 Let the nuts or seeds cool

As soon as the nuts or seeds are golden, after 2–3 minutes, transfer them to a plate so they don't continue to cook in the pan. They will become a little crisper as they cool.

Grating Nutmeg

1 Grate the nutmeg

Run a whole nutmeg over a rasp grater or specialized nutmeg grater to grate it into very fine pieces. (The flavor of freshly grated nutmeg is much better than the preground spice.)

2 Measure the grated nutmeg

Use a measuring spoon to measure out the amount needed in a recipe. A little nutmeg goes a long way, so start with the minimum amount when seasoning a dish.

Zesting Citrus

1 Wash the citrus

Before you zest an orange, lemon, or other citrus fruit, wash it well to remove any wax or chemical residue on the peel. Better yet, buy organic citrus for zesting.

2 Grate the citrus zest

Use a rasp grater or the finest rasps on a box grater-shredder to remove the colored portion of the peel, not the bitter white pith. Scrape the back of the grater clean, too.

Juicing Citrus

1 Cut the citrus in half

First press and roll the citrus fruit firmly against the counter to break some of the membranes holding in the juice. Then, using a chef's knife, cut the fruit in half crosswise.

2 Juice the citrus

To extract as much juice as possible, use a citrus reamer to pierce the membranes as you squeeze. Catch the juice in a bowl, and strain it to remove the seeds before using.

Roasting Bell Peppers

1 Line a baking sheet with foil
To roast bell peppers (capsicums) in the broiler (grill), place an oven rack as close to the heat source as possible. Line a rimmed baking sheet with aluminum foil and put the peppers on the sheet.

2 Roast the peppers
Place the sheet with the peppers under the broiler and broil (grill), turning the peppers as needed with tongs, until charred and blistered on all sides, about 15 minutes.

Working with Fresh Ginger

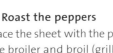

1 Peel the ginger
Using a vegetable peeler, peel away the papery brown skin from the ginger to reveal the light flesh underneath.

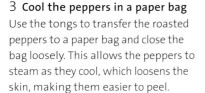

3 Cool the peppers in a paper bag
Use the tongs to transfer the roasted peppers to a paper bag and close the bag loosely. This allows the peppers to steam as they cool, which loosens the skin, making them easier to peel.

4 Peel away the skins
When the peppers are cool, remove them from the bag and use your fingers to peel and rub away as much of the charred skin as possible. Don't worry if a few bits of skin remain.

2 Chop the ginger
Using a chef's knife, cut the peeled ginger into disks, and then cut the disks into strips. Cut the strips crosswise into small pieces. To mince the pieces, rock the heel of the knife over them.

Working with Jalapeño Chiles

1 Quarter the chile lengthwise
Many cooks wear a disposable latex glove on the hand that touches the chile to prevent irritation from its potent oils. Using a paring knife, cut the chile in half, then into quarters.

2 Remove the seeds and ribs
Cut away the seeds, ribs, and stem from each chile quarter. *Capsaicin*, the compound that makes chiles hot, is concentrated in these areas; removing them lessens the heat.

Dicing Bacon

1 Slice the bacon into strips
Stack 2 or 3 bacon slices on top of one another on the cutting board and cut them lengthwise into narrow strips. Use thick-cut bacon if possible for the most uniform dice.

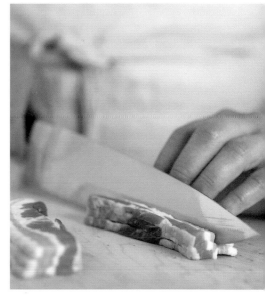

3 Slice the quarters into strips
Place the quarters, cut side up, on the cutting board. Cut into narrow strips about ⅛ inch (3 mm) wide. Take care not to pierce the latex glove.

4 Dice and mince the strips
Line up the chile strips and cut them crosswise at ⅛-inch intervals. Rest your fingertips on the top of the knife tip and rock the heel of the knife over the pieces to mince them.

2 Dice the bacon
Cut the bacon strips crosswise at ¼-inch (6-mm) intervals to create small dice.

Shucking Oysters

1 Select a type of oyster
Each oyster variety has a different flavor. Shown below are a Pacific oyster (top), a flat oyster (right), a Kumamoto oyster (bottom), and an Atlantic oyster (left). See page 138 for more on oysters.

2 Grasp the oyster
Place an oyster on a work surface and identify the flat side. Fold a thick kitchen towel in half and use it to pick up the oyster so the flat side is facing up. The towel will protect your hand.

3 Insert the knife into the hinge
Using an oyster knife, locate the hinge at the pointed end of the oyster. Insert the tip of the knife into the hinge about ½ inch (12 mm) deep.

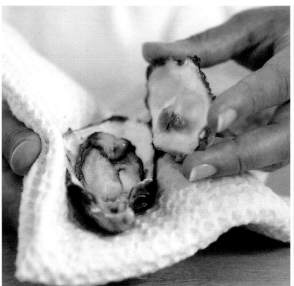

5 Detach the muscle
Run the knife all along the inside surface of the top shell to detach the muscle that connects the oyster. Be careful not to spill any of the precious juice, or oyster *liquor*.

6 Pull off the top shell
Bend the top shell of the oyster backward, snapping it off at the hinge. Discard the top shell.

7 Loosen the oyster
Run the knife along the inside surface of the bottom shell to loosen the oyster completely. Leave the oyster in this half shell. Repeat steps 2 through 7 with the remaining oysters.

4 Twist the knife

Twist and pry the knife sharply while it is still in the hinge to loosen the top shell. This will allow you to lift the oyster's top shell.

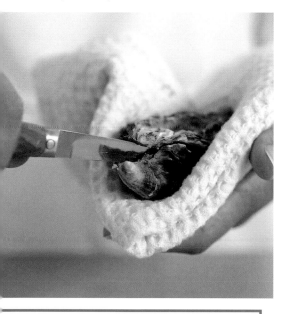

TROUBLESHOOTING

Carefully examine each oyster for cracked or broken shells; this is a sign that the oyster is dead and must be discarded. Also discard any open oysters that do not close to the touch.

Making Dried Bread Crumbs

1 Dry the bread slices

Preheat the oven to 200°F (95°C). Arrange slices of coarse country bread, such as French or Italian bread, on a rimmed baking sheet. Let the slices dry in the oven for about 1 hour.

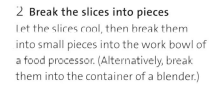

2 Break the slices into pieces

Let the slices cool, then break them into small pieces into the work bowl of a food processor. (Alternatively, break them into the container of a blender.)

3 Pulse to create crumbs

Pulse the food processor or blender until the bread pieces are ground into fine pieces. You may need to do this in batches to ensure that the crumbs have an even texture.

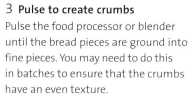

4 Pour the crumbs into a bowl

Pour the crumbs into a bowl to measure them for a recipe. If you are not using them right away, store them in an airtight container in the refrigerator for up to 1 month.

3

Dips & Spreads

Dips and spreads are an excellent place to start if you are new to making hors d'oeuvres. Many of them are easy to prepare, and you can assemble them in advance, so they will fit into any schedule. Although dips are often simple, their presentation doesn't need to be plain. You will soon learn how easy it is to spread white bean dip on cucumber slices or spoon dollops of tapenade on toasts.

White Bean Dip

Transforming dried beans into a purée is a simple process that calls for gentle simmering, followed by a short stint in a food processor. The final mixture must be smooth, light, and moist, so that the chip, toast, or other accompaniment holds up under the weight of the dip.

1 Soak the beans
Place the beans in a large colander. Sort through the beans and discard any that are wrinkled or blemished, along with any pebbles or grit. Rinse the beans well under running cold water and transfer them to a large saucepan. Add enough water to cover the beans by 2 inches (5 cm). Let the beans soak in the refrigerator for at least 8 hours or up to overnight. As the beans rehydrate, they will soften and expand, which speeds their cooking. Discard any husks that float to the top of the water. Drain the beans in the colander and rinse the pan.

2 Finely dice the shallots
If you are not sure how to dice a shallot, turn to page 38. Cut the shallots in half lengthwise and peel each half. One at a time, place the shallot halves, cut side down, on the cutting board. Alternately make a series of lengthwise cuts, parallel cuts, then crosswise cuts to create ⅛-inch (3-mm) dice. Be sure to stop just short of the root end; this holds the shallot half together as you cut.

3 Cook the beans
Return the beans to the saucepan. Add the chicken stock, diced shallots, and bay leaf. Place over high heat, cover, and bring the stock to a gentle boil, stirring occasionally. As soon as you see bubbles start to form, reduce the heat to a level where small bubbles occasionally break the surface of the liquid. Partially cover the pot and simmer gently, stirring occasionally, until the beans taste creamy in the center and are completely tender, 45–55 minutes. (If the beans are not *new crop*, that is, harvested within the last year, they may take longer to cook.) ›

For the bean dip

1 cup (7 oz/220 g) dried white beans such as Great Northern beans or cannellini beans

4 shallots, 3–4 oz (90–125 g) total weight

5¾ cups (46 fl oz/1.4 l) low-sodium chicken stock or water

1 bay leaf

1 small bunch fresh chives

4–6 sprigs fresh chervil

2 or 3 sprigs fresh tarragon

3 tablespoons extra-virgin olive oil

1½ tablespoons fresh lemon juice (page 43)

½ teaspoon kosher salt

1 tomato

2 or 3 sprigs fresh flat-leaf (Italian) parsley

For serving

Pita Crisps (page 22) or crudités such as fluted cucumber slices (page 41), green or yellow beans blanched for 3–4 minutes (page 33), or red bell pepper (capsicum) sticks (page 35)

MAKES ABOUT 3 CUPS (2 LB/1 KG), OR 6–8 SERVINGS

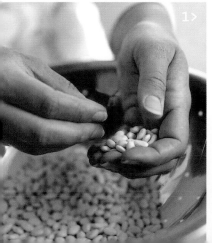

5>>

4 Snip the chives and mince the herbs

While the beans are simmering, prepare the herbs. First, snip the chives: Using kitchen scissors, snip the chive blades into tiny pieces. Measure out 2 tablespoons snipped chives. Then, mince the chervil (if you need help, turn to page 42): Remove the leaves from the chervil sprigs and discard the stems. Gather the leaves into a small pile. Holding down the knife tip with one hand, chop the chervil, moving the blade up and down in a rhythmic motion until the leaves are uniformly chopped into very fine pieces, or *minced*. Measure out 2 tablespoons minced chervil. Repeat to mince the tarragon and measure out 1 tablespoon.

5 Coarsely purée the bean mixture

When the beans are cooked, drain them through a sieve set over a large bowl to reserve the cooking liquid. Discard the bay leaf. Transfer ⅔ cup (4½ oz/140 g) of the beans to a bowl and set aside. Transfer the remaining beans to a food processor. Using brief pulses, process the beans until they are coarsely puréed, stopping occasionally to scrape down the sides of the bowl with a rubber spatula.

6 Finely purée the bean mixture

With the food processor motor running, slowly pour ½ cup (4 fl oz/125 ml) of the reserved cooking liquid through the feed tube. Stop the machine and check the purée: it should be thin and light, but thick enough to hold its shape. Add a little more of the liquid if necessary. Reserve the remaining liquid for another use. Now, process the mixture for 2–3 minutes longer, stopping occasionally to scrape down the sides of the bowl, until a fine purée forms. With the processor running, drizzle the olive oil and the lemon juice through the feed tube. Then, use the rubber spatula to scrape the purée into a bowl.

7 Add the whole beans and remaining seasonings

Add the reserved whole beans, chives, chervil, tarragon, and salt to the purée. Stir well with the rubber spatula. Cover the bowl and refrigerate for at least 5 hours or up to overnight to allow the flavors to develop. >

CHEF'S TIP
When chopping and mincing herbs, be sure to dry the rinsed herbs completely before you start to cut them. A salad spinner is a good tool to use. Wet herbs are frustrating to work with because they stick to the knife.

8 Bring the bean mixture to room temperature

Remove the bean mixture from the refrigerator about 2 hours before serving to bring it to room temperature. The flavors will be most pronounced after the chill has faded.

MAKE-AHEAD TIP

Bean dips are the perfect hors d'oeuvres to make in advance, especially since you need to soak the beans overnight. Consider making the dip 2 or even 3 days before your party to give the flavors extra time to develop. Be sure you don't add the tomato garnish until just before serving. Tomatoes turn mealy when refrigerated.

9 Prepare the tomato

If you need help seeding and dicing the tomato, turn to page 36. First, seed the tomato: Cut the tomato in half crosswise through its "equator." Hold each tomato half over a bowl and use a finger to scoop out the seed sacs and any excess liquid. Discard the seed sacs and liquid. Then, dice the tomato: Using a chef's knife, cut out the core if necessary. One at a time, place a tomato half cut side down on a cutting board and cut into slices ⅛ inch (3 mm) thick. Stack 2 or 3 slices at a time on their sides and cut into ⅛-inch strips. Finally, cut the strips crosswise into ⅛-inch dice. Stir three-fourths of the diced tomato into the bean dip.

10 Adjust the seasonings

Taste the dip. It should taste primarily of the white beans, with accents of the herbs and lemon juice. If you feel it tastes dull, stir in a small amount of salt and lemon juice until you are happy with the flavor balance. You can also add a touch more of the minced herbs if you like a stronger herbal flavor.

11 Serve the dip

Transfer the dip to a serving bowl and garnish with the remaining diced tomato. Mince the parsley and sprinkle on top. Accompany with pita crisps or with a platter of crudités. Serve right away.

Serving ideas

Part of the appeal of a creamy dip is being able to scoop it up easily from a bowl with a pita crisp, chip, or crudité. But for a more elegant presentation, you can spoon the dip into toast cups or spread it onto cucumber slices and pass them on trays, freeing your guests from crowding around a single bowl. If you prefer a dip served the traditional way, accompany it with fresh vegetables in a variety of complementary colors.

Canapés (top left)
Toast Cups (page 22) are one way to use a dip to make a canapé, a piece of bread or pastry topped with a savory spread. You can also use Pita Crisps (page 22); just place a small dollop in the center.

Assorted crudités (left)
A bountiful array of crudités (raw vegetables) or blanched vegetables for dipping will immediately draw your guests' attention. Green and yellow beans, blanched for 3–4 minutes (page 33), and slender radishes pair well with white bean dip.

Fluted cucumber slices (above)
These attractive cucumber slices (page 41) can be used as a base or served alongside for dipping.

Bean Dip Variations

After you've mastered transforming dried white beans into a creamy purée (page 51), you can apply what you've learned to a wide range of other bean varieties, including familiar pinto beans or black beans or more unusual fava beans or *edamame* (soybeans). By changing the seasonings, you can give each dip a unique ethnic accent, transforming its identity from the original French-style dip with white beans, lemon juice, and fresh tarragon and chervil to a traditional Mexican blend of black beans, lime juice, and fresh cilantro or a Japanese-inspired mix of *edamame,* rice vinegar, and fresh ginger. Each variation makes 6 to 8 servings.

Pinto Bean Dip

This traditional Tex-Mex dip is also delicious with Tortilla Chips (page 24).

Sort through and soak 1 cup (7 oz/220 g) dried pinto beans for at least 8 hours.

Next, drain the beans and add them to a saucepan with 5¾ cups (46 fl oz/1.4 l) low-sodium chicken stock, 3 whole peeled garlic cloves, 1 diced yellow onion, 1 seeded and diced small jalapeño chile, and 1 bay leaf. Simmer, partially covered and stirring occasionally, until tender, 45–55 minutes. Drain the beans, reserving the cooking liquid. Discard the bay leaf.

In a food processor, coarsely purée all the beans and vegetables. With the processor running, slowly pour ½ cup (4 fl oz/125 ml) of the cooking liquid through the feed tube and then add 3 tablespoons fresh lime juice and 2 tablespoons olive oil. When the purée is smooth, transfer it to a bowl. Stir in 1½ teaspoons kosher salt, 1½ teaspoons ground cumin, and ¼ teaspoon chipotle chile powder. Refrigerate for at least 5 hours.

When ready to serve, bring to room temperature and adjust the seasonings. Just before serving, sprinkle with ½ cup (2 oz/60 g) shredded Cheddar cheese.

Hummus

Serve with broccoli or cauliflower florets blanched for 3–5 minutes (page 33).

Sort through and soak 1 cup (7 oz/220 g) dried chickpeas (garbanzo beans) for at least 8 hours.

Next, drain the chickpeas and add them to a saucepan with 5¾ cups (46 fl oz/1.4 l) low-sodium chicken stock, 1 diced yellow onion, and 1 bay leaf. Simmer, partially covered and stirring occasionally, until tender, 45–55 minutes. Drain the beans, reserving the cooking liquid. Discard the bay leaf.

In a food processor, coarsely purée all the beans and onion. Add 2 halved large garlic cloves and process to combine. With the processor running, slowly pour ½ cup (4 fl oz/125 ml) of the cooking liquid through the feed tube and then add ⅓ cup (3 fl oz/80 ml) fresh lemon juice, ¼ cup (2½ oz/75 g) tahini, and 1 tablespoon extra-virgin olive oil. When the purée is smooth, transfer it to a bowl. Stir in 1 teaspoon *each* ground cumin and kosher salt and ⅛ teaspoon freshly ground white pepper. Refrigerate for at least 5 hours.

When ready to serve, bring to room temperature and adjust the seasonings. Just before serving, sprinkle lightly with sweet or hot paprika.

Fava Bean Dip

Pair this dip, inspired by the flavors of Tuscany, with Pita Crisps (page 22).

Sort through and soak 1 cup (7 oz/220 g) small dried split yellow fava (broad) beans for at least 8 hours.

Next, drain the beans and add them to a saucepan with 5¾ cups (46 fl oz/1.4 l) low-sodium chicken stock, 3 whole peeled garlic cloves, 1 diced yellow onion, and 1 bay leaf. Simmer, partially covered and stirring occasionally, until tender, 25–30 minutes. Drain the beans, reserving the cooking liquid. Discard the bay leaf.

In a food processor, coarsely purée all the beans and vegetables. With the processor running, slowly pour 3 tablespoons of the cooking liquid through the feed tube and then add 3 tablespoons fresh lemon juice and 2 tablespoons extra-virgin olive oil. When the purée is smooth, transfer it to a bowl. Stir in ½ cup (2 oz/60 g) freshly grated *pecorino romano* cheese, 2 tablespoons minced fresh basil, 1 tablespoon minced fresh mint, ½ teaspoon kosher salt, and ⅛ teaspoon freshly ground white pepper. Refrigerate for at least 5 hours.

When ready to serve, bring to room temperature and adjust the seasonings. Just before serving, sprinkle with 1 tablespoon minced fresh basil.

Black Bean Dip

Serve this popular Mexican-style dip with Tortilla Chips (page 24).

Sort through and soak 1 cup (7 oz/220 g) dried black beans for at least 8 hours.

Next, drain the beans and add them to a saucepan with 5¾ cups (46 fl oz/1.4 l) low-sodium chicken stock, 4 finely diced shallots, and 1 bay leaf. Simmer, partially covered and stirring occasionally, until tender, 45–55 minutes. Drain the beans, reserving the cooking liquid. Discard the bay leaf and set aside ⅔ cup (4½ oz/140 g) of the beans.

In a food processor, coarsely purée the remaining beans. Add 2 halved large garlic cloves, 2 teaspoons dried oregano, and ½ teaspoon ground cumin and process to combine. With the processor running, slowly pour ½ cup (4 fl oz/125 ml) of the cooking liquid through the feed tube and then add 3 tablespoons olive oil and 1½ tablespoons fresh lime juice. When the purée is smooth, transfer it to a bowl. Stir in 2 tablespoons minced fresh cilantro (fresh coriander) and 1 seeded and minced jalapeño chile (or to taste) and the reserved whole beans. Refrigerate for at least 5 hours.

When ready to serve, bring to room temperature. Finely dice ½ large red bell pepper (capsicum). Stir three-fourths of the pepper into the dip. Adjust the seasonings. Just before serving, sprinkle with the remaining bell pepper and 2 tablespoons minced red onion.

Cannellini Bean & Roasted Red Pepper Dip

Serve this Italian-style dip with Toasts (page 22) or with asparagus spears blanched for 3–5 minutes (page 33).

Sort through and soak 1 cup (7 oz/220 g) dried cannellini beans for at least 8 hours.

Next, drain the beans and add them to a saucepan with 5¾ cups (46 fl oz/1.4 l) low-sodium chicken stock, 1 diced yellow onion, 1 bay leaf, 2 fresh sage leaves, and ¼ teaspoon red pepper flakes. Simmer, partially covered and stirring occasionally, until tender, 45–55 minutes.

Meanwhile, preheat the oven to 350°F (180°C). Lightly coat 6 unpeeled large garlic cloves with ½ teaspoon extra-virgin olive oil and wrap in aluminum foil. Roast until tender when pierced with a knife, about 20 minutes. Unwrap, let cool, and peel off the papery skins. Drain the beans, reserving the cooking liquid. Discard the bay leaf.

In a food processor, coarsely purée all the beans and onion with the roasted garlic. With the processor running, slowly pour ½ cup (4 fl oz/125 ml) of the cooking liquid through the feed tube and then add 2 tablespoons extra-virgin olive oil and 1 tablespoon white wine vinegar. When the purée is smooth, transfer it to a bowl. Stir in 1½ teaspoons kosher salt and 1 roasted and diced large red bell pepper (capsicum) (page 44). Refrigerate for at least 5 hours.

When ready to serve, bring to room temperature and adjust the seasonings. Just before serving, sprinkle with 2 tablespoons minced fresh basil.

Edamame Dip

The Asian flavors in this dip work well with Pita Crisps (page 22) or with carrot, celery, or bell pepper (capsicum) sticks (pages 34–35).

Bring a large pot three-fourths full of water to a boil. Add 1 tablespoon kosher salt, 1 lb (500 g) thawed frozen or fresh shelled *edamame* (soybeans), and 2 peeled garlic cloves. Let the water return to a boil and cook until the beans are tender, about 3 minutes. Drain the beans, reserving the cooking liquid.

In a food processor, coarsely purée all the beans and garlic. Add ⅓ cup (1 oz/30 g) sliced green (spring) onions (white and tender green parts) and process to combine. With the processor running, slowly pour ½ cup (4 fl oz/125 ml) of the cooking liquid through the feed tube and then add 3 tablespoons peanut or soybean oil, 2 tablespoons seasoned rice vinegar, and 1 tablespoon soy sauce. Check the consistency of the dip; you may need to add a bit more of the cooking liquid. Finally, add 1 teaspoon grated fresh ginger and ½ teaspoon Asian sesame oil and process to combine. When the purée is smooth, transfer it to a bowl. Refrigerate for at least 5 hours.

When ready to serve, bring to room temperature and adjust the seasonings. Just before serving, sprinkle with 2 teaspoons toasted sesame seeds (page 42) and 1 tablespoon minced green onion.

Salsa Fresca

This fresh salsa is best in summer and early autumn when vine-ripened tomatoes are at their peak. Finely dice all the ingredients to ensure that their flavors will blend. A salsa should be more of a personal statement than a strict formula. Each time you make it, you will learn how to adjust the flavors to your personal taste.

1 Seed and dice the tomatoes
If you need help seeding and dicing the tomatoes, turn to page 36. First, seed the tomatoes: Cut each tomato in half crosswise through its "equator." Hold each tomato half over a bowl and use a finger to scoop out the seed sacs. Discard the seed sacs. Then, dice the tomatoes: Using a chef's knife, cut out the cores if necessary. One at a time, place a tomato half cut side down on a cutting board and cut into slices ¼ inch (6 mm) thick. Stack 2 or 3 slices at a time on their sides and cut into ¼-inch strips. Finally, cut the strips crosswise into ¼-inch dice. Transfer the diced tomatoes to a glass or ceramic bowl to keep your cutting area free while you work.

2 Mince the chile
If you are new to working with chiles, turn to page 45. Wear a disposable latex glove, if desired, on the hand that touches the chile, and take care not to touch your face while working. With a small sharp knife, cut the jalapeño chile lengthwise into quarters. With the tip of the knife, cut the stem, ribs, and seeds from each quarter. Slice each quarter into narrow strips about ⅛ inch (3 mm) thick. Cut the strips crosswise into ⅛-inch dice. Holding down the knife tip with one hand, continue to chop the chile, moving the blade up and down in a rhythmic motion until it is uniformly chopped into very fine pieces, or *minced*.

3 Mix the salsa
Add half of the chile, the red onion, green onion, cilantro, lime juice, and salt to the tomatoes in the bowl. Using a fork, mix the ingredients well, taking care not to crush the tomatoes.

4 Adjust the seasonings
Taste the salsa. If it is not spicy enough, add more chile. If the salsa doesn't seem fresh or acidic enough, add more lime juice. If it doesn't seem tangy enough, add more onion, or if it needs a stronger herbal note, add more cilantro. Finally, salt will heighten all the flavors, so taste again and add more if needed. Mix in each ingredient a little at a time until the flavor balance tastes right to you.

5 Serve the salsa
Transfer the mixture to a serving bowl. If possible, serve the salsa right away, as it tastes best when freshly made. It can, however, sit at room temperature for up 3 hours before serving, if necessary. Accompany with tortilla chips.

For the salsa

4 tomatoes, 1–1¼ lb (500–625 g) total weight

1 jalapeño chile, or more if desired for a hotter salsa

2 tablespoons finely diced red onion (page 38)

2 tablespoons minced green (spring) onion, white and tender green parts (page 40)

2 tablespoons minced fresh cilantro (fresh coriander) (page 42)

2 tablespoons fresh lime juice (page 43)

½ teaspoon kosher salt

For serving

Tortilla Chips (page 24)

MAKES ABOUT 2 CUPS (16 FL OZ/500 ML), OR 4–6 SERVINGS

CHEF'S TIP
Store fresh tomatoes you grow or buy at room temperature. The cold of a refrigerator robs them of both flavor and texture.

Guacamole

This creamy, nutty pale green dip should have a marked spiciness, delivered by fresh jalapeño chile, as well as a pleasant tartness from the lime. Although the avocados are cubed and then mashed (instead of blended until smooth), the texture is still velvety and rich, and the dip has sufficient body to be scooped up easily with the vegetables or chips that accompany it.

For the guacamole

2 or 3 Hass avocados, 10–12 oz (315–375 g) total weight

1 or 2 large cloves garlic, minced (page 39)

2 tablespoons minced green (spring) onion, white and tender green parts (page 40)

1 jalapeño chile, seeded, deribbed, and minced (page 45), or more if desired for a hotter guacamole

2 tablespoons minced fresh cilantro (fresh coriander) (page 42)

2 teaspoons fresh lime juice (page 43)

¼ teaspoon kosher salt

For serving

½ tomato

2 large red or yellow bell peppers (capsicums), cut into sticks (page 35) or Tortilla Chips (page 24)

MAKES ABOUT 1½ CUPS (12 FL OZ/375 ML), OR 4 SERVINGS

CHEF'S TIP

Ripe avocados can be hard to find, so plan to buy unripe avocados a few days before you need them and let them ripen at home. To hasten the ripening, place them in a paper bag with an apple or a banana. The other fruits will emit ethylene gases that speed ripening.

1 **Pit the avocados**
If you are new to working with avocados, turn to page 37. Using a chef's knife, cut each avocado in half lengthwise, cutting down to and around the pit. Gently rotate the halves in opposite directions to separate them. Carefully holding the half with the pit in one hand, strike the pit with the heel of the blade of a chef's knife, lodging it in the pit. Twist the knife and lift out the pit. To remove the pit from the knife, use your thumb and index finger to carefully push down on the pit over the dull edge of the knife.

2 **Remove the avocado from the skin**
Using a paring knife, score each half by cutting parallel lines at ¼-inch (6-mm) intervals; be careful not to cut through the skin. Turn the half 90 degrees and cut another set of parallel lines at ¼-inch intervals perpendicular to the first ones, creating squares. Use a large spoon to scoop out the avocado pieces into a glass or ceramic bowl.

3 **Mix the dip**
Add the garlic, green onion, half of the chile, the cilantro, lime juice, and salt to the avocados. Using a fork, mash the ingredients together to form a coarse paste.

4 **Adjust the seasonings**
Taste the dip. If it is not spicy enough, add more chile. If it is not tart enough or tastes flat, add more lime juice. If it lacks tang, adjust with additional green onion, or if it needs a stronger herbal flavor, mix in more cilantro. Finally, salt will heighten all the flavors, so taste again and add more if needed. Mix in any ingredient a little at a time until the flavor balance tastes right to you.

5 **Garnish and serve the dip**
Transfer the mixture to a serving bowl. If not serving right away, cover the dip with plastic wrap, pressing it directly on the surface, to prevent discoloration. Just before serving, prepare the tomato garnish. If you need help seeding and dicing the tomato half, turn to page 36. Hold the tomato half over a bowl and use a finger to scoop out the seed sacs and any excess liquid. Discard the seed sacs and liquid. Using a chef's knife, cut out the core if necessary. Place the tomato half cut side down on a cutting board and cut into slices ¼ inch thick. Stack 2 or 3 slices at a time on their sides and cut into ¼-inch strips. Finally, cut the strips crosswise into ¼-inch dice. Sprinkle the diced tomato over the guacamole. Serve right away or within 2 hours, with the bell pepper sticks or tortilla chips.

Tapenade

A classic olive spread of southern France, tapenade relies on a quartet of bold-flavored ingredients: olives, capers, anchovies, and garlic. Each one contributes its distinctive character—piquancy, saltiness, richness, texture—to the mix, which mellows nicely if made at least a day before serving.

1 Pit the olives for the spread

If you need help pitting the olives, turn to page 35. Place the olives in a locking plastic bag, force out the air, seal closed, and gently pound with a meat pounder or a rolling pin to loosen the pits. Remove the crushed olives from the bag and separate the pits from the olive flesh with your fingers. For stubborn olives, use a paring knife to cut the flesh from the pits. Double-check to make sure all the pits have been removed.

2 Mix the ingredients in a food processor

In a food processor, combine the pitted olives, capers, garlic, lemon juice, and the anchovy fillet, if using (the anchovy will add a sharp, salty flavor to the tapenade). Process the mixture with brief pulses until coarsely chopped. Stop the processor occasionally and use a rubber spatula to scrape down the sides of the work bowl. With the processor motor running, add the olive oil a little bit at a time through the feed tube in a very thin stream. When all the oil has been added, process with brief pulses, stopping occasionally to scrape down the sides of the work bowl with the rubber spatula, until the mixture forms a coarse or relatively fine purée, depending on your preference.

3 Adjust the seasonings

Taste the spread. If it tastes a bit flat, add a little more lemon juice. If you feel it needs a sharper flavor, add a few more capers or more anchovy.

4 Let the flavors marry

Transfer the tapenade to a container, cover, and refrigerate for at least 1 day or up to 2 weeks. The resting time allows all the flavors to blend and mellow.

5 Serve the spread

Remove the spread from the refrigerator about 2 hours before serving to bring it to room temperature. The flavors will be more pronounced after the chill has faded. Spread 1–2 tablespoons of the tapenade on each toast, garnish with the parsley, and arrange on a serving plate. Alternatively, transfer the spread to a serving bowl, garnish with the parsley, arrange the toasts in a napkin-lined basket, and let guests assemble their own hors d'oeuvres. Be sure to provide a small spreading knife to use for serving the tapenade.

For the tapenade

½ lb (250 g) Kalamata or Niçoise olives

1½ tablespoons brine-packed capers, rinsed and drained

1 large clove garlic, halved

1 tablespoon fresh lemon juice (page 43)

1 olive oil–packed anchovy fillet, coarsely chopped, optional

2 tablespoons extra-virgin olive oil

For serving

Toasts (page 22)

2 tablespoons coarsely chopped fresh flat-leaf (Italian) parsley (page 42)

MAKES ABOUT ¾ CUP (6 FL OZ/180 ML), OR 6–8 SERVINGS

CHEF'S TIP

Tapenade is an easy hors d'oeuvre to make and serve, but it can be used in other ways, too. For a weeknight supper, spoon a small dollop onto simply cooked chicken, fish, or vegetables to perk up the flavor.

Mushroom Pâté

When spread, this elegant pâté reveals an attractive pattern of mushroom and leek slices. Sautéing the fresh mushrooms enriches their flavor, while using dried mushrooms contributes a pleasing earthiness to the pâté. I like to bake the pâté in a handsome terrine and then serve it in the same dish for an easy presentation.

For the vegetables

½ oz (15 g) dried porcini (ceps) or other dried mushrooms

¾ cup (6 fl oz/180 ml) hot water

3 tablespoons extra-virgin olive oil

2 tablespoons unsalted butter

¾ lb (375 g) fresh shiitake or cremini mushrooms, each about 1½ inches (4 cm) in diameter, brushed clean, stems removed for shiitake or stems trimmed for cremini, and thinly sliced

2 large shallots, diced (page 38)

3 large cloves garlic, coarsely chopped (page 39)

2 tablespoons soy sauce

1 small leek, white and pale green parts, thinly sliced (page 40)

1 teaspoon champagne vinegar

¼ teaspoon kosher salt

For the pâté mixture

¾ cup (6 fl oz/180 ml) heavy (double) cream

1 teaspoon champagne vinegar

⅛ teaspoon freshly grated nutmeg (page 43)

¼ teaspoon freshly ground pepper

2 large eggs

2 tablespoons coarsely chopped fresh tarragon (page 42)

1 tablespoon snipped fresh chives

Unsalted butter for preparing the terrine

For serving

Toasts (page 22) or crackers

MAKES 8–10 SERVINGS

1 Prepare the dried mushrooms
Rinse the dried mushrooms and place in a small bowl. Add the hot water and let the mushrooms soak until softened, about 30 minutes. Strain the mushrooms through a sieve lined with a double layer of cheesecloth (muslin) set over a bowl. Chop the mushrooms, removing any tough stems, and set aside. Reserve the liquid.

2 Cook the mushrooms and the leek
Place a large frying pan over medium-high heat and add 2 tablespoons of the olive oil and the butter. When the butter and oil are hot, add the fresh mushrooms and cook, stirring often, until softened, 3–4 minutes. Raise the heat to high, add the strained mushroom liquid, the shallots, garlic, soy sauce, and soaked mushrooms. Cook until most of the liquid has evaporated, 3–4 minutes. Heat the remaining 1 tablespoon oil in another frying pan over medium-low heat. When hot, add the leek and vinegar, cover, and cook, stirring occasionally, until the leek is tender, 10–15 minutes. Add the salt, remove from the heat, and let cool slightly.

3 Preheat the oven and assemble the pâté
Preheat the oven to 350°F (180°C). Remove 1¼ cups (8 oz/250 g) of the mushroom mixture from the large frying pan and set it aside. Transfer the remaining mushroom mixture to a food processor and pulse briefly until finely chopped. Add the cream, vinegar, nutmeg, and pepper and process until a fine purée forms. Taste and adjust the seasonings. Add the eggs and process until they are completely incorporated. Add the tarragon and chives and pulse 2 or 3 times to mince the herbs. Transfer the mixture to a bowl and stir in the reserved mushroom mixture and the cooked leek.

4 Bake the pâté
Coat the sides and bottom of an ovenproof 4-cup (32–fl oz/1-l) porcelain or earthenware terrine with the butter. Add the pâté mixture and press down with a rubber spatula. Cover with aluminum foil, place in a deep roasting pan, and pour boiling water into the pan to reach three-fourths of the way up the sides of the terrine. Bake for 1 hour and remove the foil. Continue to bake until the pâté looks puffed, is just firm to the touch, and a cake tester inserted into the center comes out clean, about 15 minutes longer. Remove the terrine from the pan and let cool for 45 minutes. Refrigerate for at least 5 hours, or preferably overnight, to firm.

5 Serve the pâté
Remove the terrine from the refrigerator 30 minutes before serving. Provide a small knife for spreading the pâté onto the toasts or crackers.

Cold Hors d'Oeuvres

Once you've mastered dips and spreads, you will be ready to move on to the classics in this chapter, many of which can be prepared in advance. You will learn some new, more complex techniques, such as piping cheese fillings and finely dicing raw fish, but you will also discover some simple recipes—spiced nuts, prosciutto-wrapped figs— that come together quickly and easily.

Stuffed Vegetables with Herbed Cheese Filling

This cheese filling combines the sharp flavor of blue cheese, the natural richness of cream cheese, and the fresh taste of minced herbs. It flows easily through a pastry bag, creating attractive rosettes on whichever vegetable you choose. A garnish of pine nuts adds a bit of texture and flavor.

1 Decide which vegetable to prepare

Select the vegetable that best suits the style of your get-together or season. Cherry tomatoes are perfect summertime hors d'oeuvres, when they are at their sweetest. Belgian endive is a classic choice, ideal for more formal entertaining. Small potatoes have a more rustic character well suited to casual gatherings. If you are feeling ambitious and expecting many guests, make a large platter with all three vegetables—just triple the amount of ingredients for the filling and garnish.

2 Prepare the tomatoes, if using

Set a large cooling rack over a rimmed baking sheet. Pull off any stem still attached to each tomato. The tops of the tomatoes are flatter than the bottoms, so the tomatoes are filled upside down, allowing them to rest on their tops. Using a paring knife, cut as thin a slice as possible off the rounded bottom of each tomato. Stand the tomatoes on their stem ends. If any tomato wobbles, cut a thin slice off the top as well. Using a tomato corer or paring knife, and working with 1 tomato at a time, hold it over a bowl, insert the corer or knife into the bottom end, and twist to release the seed sacs from the tomato's interior. Using a finger, scoop out any remaining seeds and excess liquid, leaving a shell of tomato flesh. Turn the shells upside down on the cooling rack to drain for at least 15 minutes or up to 2 hours before filling.

3 Prepare the endive, if using

One at a time, place the endive heads on a cutting board and, using a paring knife, cut off the bases; this will release the outer leaves. Remove 24 leaves from the endives, using the larger leaves from each head and slicing off more of the bottoms as necessary to pull the leaves off easily. Rinse the leaves, dry well with paper towels, wrap in dry paper towels, place in a plastic bag, and refrigerate until filling or up to 6 hours. ▸

CHEF'S TIP

When freshly grating a small amount of spice such as nutmeg, keep the following guideline in mind: 10–12 gratings equals about ⅛ teaspoon.

For the vegetables

24 large cherry tomatoes, each about 1 inch (2.5 cm) in diameter, if using

2 or 3 large heads green or red Belgian endive (chicory/witloof), if using

24 very small potatoes, each about 1½ inches (4 cm) in diameter, unpeeled, if using

⅛ teaspoon kosher salt or sea salt, if using the potatoes

For the garnish

3 tablespoons pine nuts

For the filling

7–10 blades fresh chives

6–8 sprigs fresh dill

6–8 leaves fresh basil

⅓ lb (155 g) mild blue cheese such as Gorgonzola *dolcelatte*, at room temperature

⅓–½ lb (155–250 g) cream cheese, at room temperature

2 teaspoons sherry vinegar

1 teaspoon Dijon mustard

1 teaspoon extra-virgin olive oil

1 teaspoon fresh lemon juice (page 43)

⅛ teaspoon freshly grated nutmeg (page 43)

Kosher salt, if needed

MAKES ABOUT 1¼ CUPS (10 FL OZ/310 ML) FILLING, OR 4–6 SERVINGS

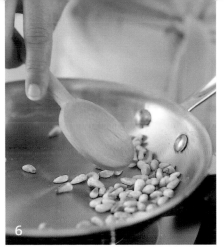

4 Cook the potatoes, if using

Place a steamer basket in a saucepan and add water until it almost reaches the bottom of the basket. Remove the basket. Bring the water to a boil over medium-high heat. As soon as you see large bubbles forming in the water, place the basket in the pan and add the potatoes. Cover the pan and steam the potatoes until they are easily pierced with a knife, 20–25 minutes. Remove the basket from the pan and let the potatoes stand until cool.

5 Hollow out the potatoes, if using

Using a paring knife, cut a very thin slice off one rounded side of each potato, so it will stand upright. Using a melon baller or a small spoon, scoop out a little flesh from the other side to create a small hollow. Sprinkle the potatoes with the salt.

6 Toast the pine nuts

For more details on toasting nuts, turn to page 42. Spread the pine nuts in a dry frying pan. Place over medium heat and toast, stirring frequently, until medium brown and fragrant, about 3 minutes. Don't walk away; the nuts burn easily. Immediately transfer the nuts to a plate to stop the cooking. When the nuts are completely cool, chop them coarsely with a chef's knife and set aside.

7 Snip the chives and mince the herbs for the filling

When you have finished chopping the pine nuts, prepare the herbs. First, snip the chives: Using kitchen scissors, snip the chive blades into tiny pieces. Measure out 2 teaspoons snipped chives. Then, mince the dill (if you need help, turn to page 42): Remove the leaves from the dill sprigs and discard the stems. Gather the leaves into a small pile. Holding down the knife tip with one hand, chop the dill, moving the blade up and down in a rhythmic motion until the leaves are uniformly chopped into very fine pieces, or *minced*. Measure out 1 tablespoon minced dill. Repeat to mince the basil and measure out 1 tablespoon.

8 Make the filling

First, taste the blue cheese; if it is particularly strong, you may want to use a little less blue cheese and a little more cream cheese. In a large bowl, use a fork to mix the blue and cream cheeses together until completely smooth. Add the vinegar, mustard, olive oil, and lemon juice and stir until well blended. Add the chives, dill, basil, and nutmeg and again stir until well blended. Taste the filling; it should be mildly pungent from the blue cheese, with tangy accents of mustard, vinegar, lemon juice, and herbs. If you feel the filling tastes dull, stir in a pinch of salt or a small amount of any of the filling ingredients until you are happy with the flavor balance.

9 Assemble a pastry bag

If you are new to using a pastry (piping) bag, turn to page 30. Fit a pastry bag with a star tip and fill the bag with the filling. Set the bag aside while you ready the vegetables. >

10 **Fill and garnish the tomatoes, if using**
Turn the tomatoes hollow side up on a flat work surface. Twist the top of the pastry bag where the filling ends so you will be able to control the bag, and then secure the twisted top with one hand. Guide the tip with the index finger and thumb of the other hand, positioning the bag just above a tomato. Apply gentle pressure with the hand at the top of the bag to pipe a rosette of filling into the tomato. When the opening is filled, release the pressure, twirl and lift the bag away, and move to the next tomato. You may need to move your hand to hold onto the tomato as you lift the bag to keep the tomato steady. Repeat until all the tomatoes are filled. Garnish with the chopped pine nuts and transfer to a serving platter.

11 **Fill and garnish the endive leaves, if using**
Arrange the endive leaves on a flat work surface. Twist the top of the pastry bag where the filling ends so you will be able to control the bag, and then secure the twisted top with one hand. Guide the tip with the index finger and thumb of the other hand, positioning the bag just above a leaf. Apply gentle pressure with the hand at the top of the bag to pipe a rosette of filling into the wide end of each leaf. When the end is filled, release the pressure, twirl and lift the bag away, and move to the next leaf. You may need to move your hand to hold onto the leaf as you lift the bag to keep the leaf steady. Repeat until all the endive leaves are filled. Garnish with the chopped pine nuts and transfer to a serving platter. If you like, arrange the leaves in a spoke pattern.

12 **Fill and garnish the potatoes, if using**
Arrange the potatoes hollow side up on a flat work surface. Twist the top of the pastry bag where the filling ends so you will be able to control the bag, and then secure the twisted top with one hand. Guide the tip with the index finger and thumb of the other hand, positioning the bag above a potato. Apply gentle pressure with the hand at the top of the bag to pipe a rosette of filling into the hollow of the potato. When the hollow is filled, release the pressure, twirl and lift the bag away, and move to the next potato. You may need to move your hand to hold onto the potato as you lift the bag to keep the potato steady. Repeat until all the potatoes are filled. Garnish with the chopped pine nuts and transfer to a serving platter.

MAKE-AHEAD TIP
The filling can be prepared up to 2 days in advance and refrigerated. Bring to room temperature before using. The tomatoes and potatoes can be filled and garnished up to 2 hours in advance and kept at room temperature until serving. However, don't fill and garnish the endive leaves until just before serving, or the leaves will lose their crispness.

Finishing touches

Crowning an hors d'oeuvre with a fresh herb sprig is one of the easiest ways to add a garnish. The examples shown here, chives, basil, and dill, are three common choices, but any fresh herb used in the recipe will work. Here, the herbs may replace or be used in addition to the chopped pine nuts in the recipe on page 69. The best part is all of these simple garnishes can be eaten right along with the hors d'oeuvres they decorate.

Chives (top left)
A garnish of chives adds an architectural element along with a mild onionlike flavor. Crisscrossing the delicate blades is a classic presentation.

Basil (left)
If your hors d'oeuvre recipe calls for fresh basil, seek out the smallest leaves and save them for the garnish. You'll find clusters of these tiny leaves toward the tops of sprigs.

Dill (above)
Feathery dill is among the prettiest of all herb garnishes, and its flavor is a particularly good match for recipes using smoked salmon or sour cream. Use kitchen scissors to snip off the finest fronds.

Stuffed Vegetable Variations

Vegetables stuffed with an herb-flecked creamy cheese filling is an hors d'oeuvre menu mainstay. After you've mastered piping the cheese filling into the cold vegetables on page 69, you may also want to add some new fillings to your repertory to vary your presentation. Goat cheese mixed with sun-dried tomatoes is more rustic, while rosettes of rich salmon mousse deliver a touch of luxury. And there's no reason the filling needs to be piped. Four of these choices (including one warm option) offer easy ideas for fillings that can be spooned into the vegetables, reducing preparation time. Each variation makes 4 to 6 servings.

Cherry Tomatoes with Goat Cheese Filling

The distinct, earthy flavor of fresh goat cheese stars in this filling. A garnish of sun-dried tomato adds a nice touch of flavor and color.

Hollow out 24 large cherry tomatoes, each about 1 inch (2.5 cm) in diameter, and set them upside down on a rack to drain.

Make the filling: Use a fork to combine ½ lb (250 g) fresh goat cheese with 2–3 tablespoons whole milk, adding just enough milk to make the cheese thin enough to pipe. Add 2 tablespoons minced fresh marjoram, 2 tablespoons snipped fresh chives, ¼ teaspoon kosher salt, and ¼ teaspoon freshly ground pepper and mix well. Adjust the seasonings.

Have ready 6 oil-packed sun-dried tomatoes, each cut into 4 thin pieces.

Fit a pastry bag with a star tip, fill it with the goat cheese filling, then pipe it into each hollowed-out tomato. Garnish each filled cherry tomato with 1 piece sun-dried tomato.

Cherry Tomatoes with Salmon Mousse Filling

Salmon mousse studded with dill and capers is a nice partner for sweet tomatoes. It also pairs well with potatoes or endive leaves.

Hollow out 24 large cherry tomatoes, each about 1 inch (2.5 cm) in diameter, and set them upside down on a rack to drain.

Make the filling: Cut ¼ lb (125 g) Gravlax (page 87) or smoked salmon into large pieces and place in the work bowl of a food processor fitted with the metal blade. Add 2 oz (60 g) room-temperature cream cheese, 3 tablespoons sour cream, ½ teaspoon fresh lemon juice, and 1 tablespoon coarsely chopped fresh dill. Process until a smooth purée with tiny dill flecks forms, stopping occasionally to scrape down the sides of the work bowl. Stir in 1 tablespoon snipped fresh chives. Adjust the seasonings.

Have ready 24 rinsed and drained brine-packed capers and 24 fresh dill fronds.

Fit a pastry bag with a star tip, fill it with the salmon filling, and then pipe it into each hollowed-out tomato. Garnish each filled cherry tomato with 1 caper and 1 dill frond.

Endive Leaves with Curried Shrimp Filling

This lightly spiced filling, with a hint of curry, is an irresistible combination with sweet shrimp and crunchy endive leaves.

Separate the leaves from 2 or 3 large heads green or red Belgian endive (chicory/witloof).

Make the filling: In a small bowl, combine 3 tablespoons mayonnaise and 1 teaspoon curry powder. Add 1 cup (8 oz/250 g) diced cooked shrimp (prawns) and ¼ cup (1½ oz/45 g) finely diced celery and stir to combine. Adjust the seasonings, adding a pinch of kosher salt if needed.

In a dry frying pan over medium heat, toast 3 tablespoons slivered blanched almonds and set aside to cool. Coarsely chop the cooled nuts.

Spoon the filling into the endive leaves, using the bottom of the spoon to press the filling into the leaves so it doesn't fall out. Garnish the filled leaves with the chopped almonds and 2 tablespoons minced fresh cilantro (fresh coriander).

Endive Leaves with Smoked Chicken Filling

A filling of smoked chicken, asparagus, and radicchio beautifully complements the mildly bitter endive.

Separate the leaves from 2 or 3 large heads green or red Belgian endive (chicory/witloof).

Make the filling: Snap off the tough ends of 6 asparagus spears. Blanch the asparagus for 3–5 minutes (see page 33) and chop as finely as possible. Transfer to a bowl. Add 1¾ cups (8 oz/250 g) finely diced smoked chicken breast, ⅓ cup (2½ fl oz/ 75 ml) mayonnaise, ⅓ cup (¾ oz/20 g) minced radicchio, 2 tablespoons minced green (spring) onion (white and tender green parts), 2 tablespoons minced fresh basil, 2 tablespoons minced fresh tarragon, 1 tablespoon walnut oil, 1 teaspoon fresh lemon juice, 1 teaspoon kosher salt, and ⅛ teaspoon freshly ground white pepper and mix well. Adjust the seasonings.

In a dry frying pan over medium heat, toast 3 tablespoons pine nuts and set aside to cool. Coarsely chop the cooled nuts.

Spoon the filling into the endive leaves, using the bottom of the spoon to press the filling into the leaves so it doesn't fall out. Garnish the filled leaves with the chopped pine nuts.

Potatoes with Vegetable, Olive & Pine Nut Filling

This rustic filling is a fresh-tasting alternative to a smooth cheese-based one.

Cook and hollow out 24 very small potatoes, each about 1½ inches (4 cm) in diameter.

Make the filling: Blanch 8 trimmed green beans for 3–4 minutes (see page 33). Pat the beans dry, mince, and transfer to a small bowl. Add 2 seeded and finely diced tomatoes, 10 pitted and finely diced Kalamata olives, 1 minced shallot, and 2 tablespoons minced fresh basil. Transfer the mixture to a sieve set over a bowl or the sink for 15–20 minutes to drain any excess liquid. Return the mixture to the bowl.

Make a vinaigrette: In another small bowl, whisk together 1 tablespoon fresh lemon juice, 1 teaspoon Dijon mustard, ¼ teaspoon kosher salt, and ⅛ teaspoon freshly ground pepper. Gradually whisk in 2 tablespoons extra-virgin olive oil and 1 tablespoon walnut oil until well blended. Adjust the seasonings.

In a dry frying pan over medium heat, toast 3 tablespoons pine nuts and set aside to cool. Coarsely chop the cooled nuts.

Brush each potato with some of the vinaigrette, then stir just enough of the vinaigrette into the filling to coat the vegetables lightly. Spoon the filling into the potatoes. Garnish the filled potatoes with the chopped pine nuts.

Warm Mushrooms with Herbed Cheese Filling

This warm hors d'oeuvre suits nearly any autumn menu.

Preheat the oven to 400°F (200°C). Break off the stems of 24 fresh cremini mushrooms, each about 1¾ inches (4.5 cm) in diameter. Pour 3 tablespoons extra-virgin olive oil into a baking dish large enough to hold the mushrooms in a single layer. Turn each mushroom in the oil to coat, then arrange them, rounded side up, in the dish. Bake the mushrooms until just tender, about 10 minutes. Remove from the oven, turn the mushrooms cavity side up in the dish, and set aside. (Let the mushrooms rest at room temperature for up to 3 hours if you need to make them ahead.)

Make the filling: In a bowl, use a fork to mix ⅓ lb (155 g) room-temperature mild blue cheese and ⅓–½ lb (155–250 g) room-temperature cream cheese until completely smooth. Stir in 2 teaspoons sherry vinegar, 1 teaspoon Dijon mustard, 1 teaspoon extra-virgin olive oil, and 1 teaspoon fresh lemon juice until blended. Add 2 teaspoons snipped fresh chives, 1 tablespoon minced fresh dill, 1 tablespoon minced fresh basil, and ⅛ teaspoon freshly grated nutmeg and stir to blend. Adjust the seasonings, adding a pinch of kosher salt if needed.

Spoon a thin layer of filling into each mushroom. Sprinkle them evenly with 1 tablespoon freshly grated Parmigiano-Reggiano cheese. Bake until the cheese melts and browns, about 20 minutes. Serve right away, directly from the dish.

Blini with Caviar

Tender, lightly browned blini (yeast-raised buckwheat pancakes) are a practical and pleasantly tangy vehicle for enjoying the flavorful interplay of caviar and crème fraîche, a traditional pairing. The richly topped blini are usually cocktail-party fare but are a welcome sight at brunch, too.

1 Proof the yeast for the sponge

Pour warm tap water into a measuring cup. Using an instant-read thermometer, check the water temperature; it should register 100°F (38°C). Using a fork or small whisk, mix the yeast and brown sugar in a small bowl. Pour in enough of the warm water, 2–3 tablespoons, to make a thick paste and whisk until smooth. (The yeast will dissolve more readily if it is first mixed to a paste.) Whisk in the remaining warm water and let the yeast mixture stand for about 10 minutes. It will start to bubble and thicken.

2 Make the sponge

Making a *sponge* is an important first step in many batters leavened with yeast because it increases the fermentation period, allowing the development of special acids that give the batter a tangy flavor. In a medium bowl, use a whisk to mix together the ¼ cup buckwheat flour and ¼ cup cake flour. Now, begin pouring in the liquid, adding it in stages to avoid lumps. First, pour in only enough milk, about 3 tablespoons, to make a thick paste and whisk until completely smooth. Whisk in the remaining milk, stirring constantly until smooth, then whisk in the yeast mixture until smooth. Cover the sponge with plastic wrap and let it stand at room temperature until it thickens and bubbles vigorously and develops a slightly sour smell, which is characteristic of fermenting yeast, 2–3 hours. The sponge will rise more quickly on a warm day, more slowly on a cool day.

3 Separate the eggs for the batter

Take 2 eggs from the refrigerator (they are easiest to separate when cold). Have 2 small bowls and a regular mixing bowl or the bowl of a stand mixer ready. Crack the side of 1 egg sharply on a flat surface, rather than on the rim of a bowl. (This will reduce the chance of shell fragments.) Working over the first small bowl, pass the yolk back and forth between the shell halves, allowing the white to drop into the bowl. If the yolk breaks and gets into the white, start fresh with a new egg. (Even a speck of yolk will prevent the whites from whipping up properly.) Drop the yolk into the second small bowl. Transfer the white to the regular mixing bowl or the bowl of the stand mixer. Repeat with the remaining egg. Let the whites stand until they come to room temperature, about 30 minutes (they will whip up more quickly when they are at room temperature). Set the yolks aside.

4 Melt the butter

In a small saucepan over medium heat, melt the 2 tablespoons butter. Remove from the heat and set aside to cool. It's important for the butter to be at room temperature so it won't cook the eggs or curdle the milk. >

For the sponge

¼ cup (2 fl oz/60 ml) warm water

1 package (2½ teaspoons) active dry yeast

1 teaspoon firmly packed dark brown sugar

¼ cup (1½ oz/45 g) buckwheat flour

¼ cup (1 oz/30 g) cake (soft-wheat) flour

1 cup (8 fl oz/250 ml) whole or low-fat milk, at room temperature

For the batter

2 cold large eggs

2 tablespoons unsalted butter

½ cup (3 oz/90 g) buckwheat flour

½ cup (2 oz/60 g) cake (soft-wheat) flour

⅓ cup (3 oz/90 g) sour cream, at room temperature

1 scant teaspoon kosher salt

1 tablespoon minced fresh dill (page 42)

⅛ teaspoon cream of tartar

For cooking

About 6 tablespoons (3 oz/90 g) unsalted butter

For serving

About 1 cup (8 oz/250 g) crème fraîche or sour cream

½–¾ lb (250–375 g) caviar or other fish roe (see page 81)

¼ cup (⅓ oz/10 g) minced fresh dill (page 42) or snipped chives, optional

MAKES ABOUT 64 BLINI, OR 4–6 SERVINGS

5>>

5 Mix the batter

In a clean bowl, using a clean, dry whisk, combine the ½ cup buckwheat flour and ½ cup cake flour. Pour half the sponge into the flour mixture and whisk to make a thick, smooth paste. Whisk in the remaining sponge. Add the cooled melted butter, the sour cream, salt, and dill and whisk to combine. Whisk the reserved egg yolks into the batter.

6 Beat the egg whites

Add the cream of tartar to the egg whites. The cream of tartar will help stabilize the whites and increase their volume. Using a balloon whisk or a handheld electric mixer, beat the egg whites on medium speed until soft peaks form that hold their shape when the whisk or beaters are lifted. Do not overbeat.

7 Fold the egg whites into the batter

Using a rubber spatula, scoop up one-fourth of the beaten egg whites and place on top of the batter. Using the spatula, cut straight down through the egg whites and batter to the bottom of the bowl. Turn the spatula so that it slides along the bottom of the bowl and up one side, lifting a portion of the batter up over the egg whites. Give the bowl a quarter turn and repeat the cutting, scraping, and lifting technique until the ingredients are evenly blended. (Lightening the batter first with only one-fourth of the egg whites makes it easier to incorporate the rest of the ingredients without deflating the whites.) Next, pour the lightened batter over the remaining egg whites and repeat the folding procedure until no trace of unincorporated egg white remains. ➤

MAKE-AHEAD TIP

Once the batter has completed rising in step 8, it can be refrigerated overnight or for up to 3 days. Let it stand at room temperature for 1½–2 hours before cooking the blini.

8 Let the batter rise
Cover the bowl with plastic wrap and let the batter rest at room temperature until it puffs and bubbles. This rising time, or *fermentation*, can take 4–5 hours, during which it produces the elements that flavor the batter. Since the batter requires such a long time to rise, plan your schedule accordingly. You may need to prepare it early in the day.

CHEF'S TIP
Caviar is ideally served in a dish especially designed for its service. The top part, a concave bowl that holds the roe, sits over a second vessel filled with shaved ice to keep the caviar cold. Purists serve caviar with a special spoon made of mother-of-pearl or natural bone so no metal contaminates the flavor of the precious eggs.

9 Cook the blini
Place a rimmed baking sheet in the oven and preheat the oven to 200°F (95°C). Preheat a large frying pan or a cast-iron griddle over medium heat. When a drop of water dances on the surface, add about 2 tablespoons of the butter. When the butter has melted, use a measuring spoon or small ladle to pour about 1 tablespoon batter into the pan. The batter will spread out to form a 2-inch (5-cm) pancake. Continue adding the batter to make as many blini as you can without them touching. (If they do touch, you can separate them with the edge of a spatula.) Cook until bubbles appear on the surface of the blini, the pancakes look opaque, and the bottoms are brown, about 3 minutes. Using a wide, thin-lipped spatula, flip the blini over and cook until brown on the second sides, about 2 minutes longer. Transfer to the tray in the preheated oven to keep warm. Repeat with the remaining batter, adding additional butter to the pan when the pan looks dry.

10 Serve the blini
Arrange the blini on a serving platter. Spoon a dab of crème fraîche on each pancake. Top with a spoonful or so of caviar and a few sprinkles of minced dill, if using. Serve right away.

Serving ideas

Although they are the most traditional, beluga, osetra, and sevruga caviars are not the only possible caviars to serve with blini. You may want to try a different fish roe, such as golden salmon or whitefish roe or trout eggs. If you have the space, create a blini buffet with a selection of choices so people can pick their own accompaniments. If you or some of your guests don't care for caviar, serve cured salmon, such as gravlax, as well.

Salmon roe (top left)
The larger, jewel-like roe of salmon is a dramatic alternative to the rich dark grains of "true" caviar, which come from sturgeon.

Blini buffet (left)
For do-it-yourself hors d'oeuvres, include small bowls of minced dill or chives, chopped hard-boiled egg, crème fraîche or sour cream, and one or two types of caviar. Serve the caviar over ice and keep it covered until serving to prevent it from drying out.

Cured salmon (above)
Gravlax (page 87) is another delicious choice for blini. Serve with thinly sliced red onion and capers—both pair nicely with the cured fish.

Tuna Tartare with Lemon & Tarragon

The term *tartare* is used to describe fish or meat that is served raw. The key to good tuna tartare, in addition to impeccably fresh fish, is a balance of color, texture, and spice. Here, cucumber provides both color and crispness, while mustard, lemon, and fresh tarragon and chives complement the fish without overpowering it.

1 Finely dice the cucumber
If you are not sure how to dice the cucumber, turn to page 41. Using a vegetable peeler, peel the cucumber piece. Halve the piece lengthwise and scoop out any seeds with a small spoon or melon baller. Using a chef's knife, cut each half lengthwise into slices ⅛ inch (3 mm) thick. Then, cut each slice into strips ⅛ inch wide. Finally, cut across the strips to create ⅛-inch dice.

2 Finely dice the shallot
If you are not sure how to dice the shallot, turn to page 38. Cut the shallot in half lengthwise and peel each half. One at a time, place the shallot halves cut side down on the cutting board. Alternately make a series of lengthwise cuts, parallel cuts, and then crosswise cuts to create ⅛-inch dice. Be sure to stop just short of the root end; this holds the shallot half together as you cut.

3 Snip the chives
Using kitchen scissors, snip the chive blades into tiny pieces. (It's best to use scissors rather than a knife for this task; a knife can smash the chives.) Measure out 1 tablespoon snipped chives.

4 Mince the tarragon
If you need help mincing the tarragon, turn to page 42. Remove the leaves from the tarragon sprigs and discard the stems. Gather the leaves into a small pile. Holding down the tip of the chef's knife with one hand, chop the tarragon, moving the blade up and down in a rhythmic motion until the leaves are uniformly chopped into very fine pieces, or *minced*. Measure out 1 tablespoon minced tarragon.

5 Rinse and trim the fish
Rinse the fish and pat dry with paper towels. Using a small, sharp knife, remove any white tendons, connective tissue, and dark spots. (There should be very few imperfections in fish of this quality.) >

For the tartare

3-inch (7.5-cm) piece English (hothouse) cucumber

1 shallot

7–10 blades fresh chives

6–8 sprigs fresh tarragon

9–10 oz (280–315 g) sashimi-grade yellowfin or bluefin tuna fillet

1 tablespoon fresh lemon juice (page 43)

½ teaspoon Dijon mustard

½ teaspoon kosher salt

2 tablespoons extra-virgin olive oil

For serving

Potato Chips (page 26) or Toasts (page 22)

MAKES ABOUT 1½ CUPS, OR 4–6 SERVINGS

CHEF'S TIP
Seek out a reputable fishmonger in your area, so you can purchase the freshest, best-quality fish available. I often visit Japanese fish markets, where I can buy fish that is of the same standard of excellence used by chefs for sashimi and sushi. For tartare, use only sushi- or sashimi-grade fish and be sure to use it the same day you buy it.

6 Finely dice the fish

With a chef's knife or sharp slicing knife, cut the tuna fillet lengthwise into slices ⅛ inch (3 mm) thick. Lay each slice flat and cut it lengthwise into strips ⅛ inch wide. Then cut across the strips to create ⅛-inch dice. Carefully dicing the fish by hand gives it a much more pleasing texture than chopping with a food processor. Place the tuna in a small bowl. If you want to prepare the tuna ahead, cover the bowl with plastic wrap and refrigerate for up to 4 hours.

7 Mix the tartare

If you have refrigerated the fish, remove it from the refrigerator 15 minutes before serving. Pour the lemon juice into a small glass bowl and whisk in the mustard, salt, chives, and tarragon until well combined. Whisk in the olive oil in a thin stream and continue whisking until the mixture is well blended and slightly thickened. Stir in the cucumber and shallot. Add the cucumber mixture to the fish and mix well with a spoon. Don't mix the fish and other ingredients together any sooner, or the fish will "cook" in the acidic lemon juice, and the tartare will lose its freshness and texture and become soggy.

8 Adjust the seasonings

Taste the tartare; it should taste primarily of the meaty tuna, with accents of cucumber, shallot, herbs, and lemon. If it tastes a little dull, stir in a small amount of salt or lemon juice. If you feel the tartare needs more zip, mix in a touch more herbs or mustard until you are happy with the flavor balance.

9 Serve the tartare

Place the tartare in a serving bowl and accompany with a small serving spoon. Place the bowl on a large platter and surround with the potato chips or toasts. Alternatively, use a small spoon to spread the tartare on the toasts and arrange them on a platter. (You don't want to do this with the potato chips, as they will become soggy.)

CHEF'S TIP

For an alternative, more formal way to serve tartare, spoon the tartare into a 2½-inch (6-cm) round pastry cutter set on a serving platter. Pack it down with a spoon and then gently remove the cutter. Arrange the accompaniments around the tartare.

Tartare Variations

The flavor of sea-fresh fish is the base for an exquisite hors d'oeuvre when the fish is finely diced and mixed with a combination of carefully selected seasonings. The recipes below all reflect a well-chosen balance of flavors, textures, and colors, featuring fresh herbs such as cilantro or fennel fronds, acidic ingredients such as lime juice or rice vinegar, and textural counterpoints such as avocado or fennel bulb. Also, tuna is not your only choice: salmon makes delicious tartare, too. As you learned from making the tuna tartare on page 83, it's important to mix the fish with the seasonings just before serving. Each variation makes 4 to 6 servings.

Tuna Tartare with Lime & Cilantro

This tartare recalls ceviche with its Latin flavor profile. Serve with Tortilla Chips (page 24).

Rinse, trim, and finely dice a 9–10 oz (280–315 g) sashimi-grade yellowfin or bluefin tuna fillet.

Peel the husk from 2 tomatillos and carefully rinse off the sticky residue that covers the skin. Use a paring knife to cut out the cores, then finely dice the tomatillos.

Next, pour 1 tablespoon fresh lime juice into a small bowl and whisk in ¼ teaspoon kosher salt. Whisk in 2 tablespoons extra-virgin olive oil in a thin stream until slightly thickened. Stir in 1 seeded and minced jalapeño chile (or to taste), 2 tablespoons minced red onion, 2 tablespoons minced fresh cilantro (fresh coriander), 1 tablespoon rinsed and drained brine-packed capers, and the diced tomatillos.

Just before serving, stir ½ cup (2½ oz/ 75 g) diced avocado into the tomatillo mixture. Gently mix in the diced tuna. Adjust the seasonings and serve.

Salmon Tartare with Fennel & Lemon

Serve this delicate tartare with Pita Chips (page 22) made with fennel seeds or with Toasts (page 22).

Rinse and trim a 9–10 oz (280–315 g) never-frozen, skinned wild salmon fillet. Pull out any pin bones with small tweezers and finely dice the fish.

Cut the fronds from the stalks of 1 fennel bulb. Mince and measure out 1 tablespoon fennel fronds; set aside. Finely dice the fennel bulb and measure out ⅓ cup (2 oz/60 g). Reserve any remaining fennel or fronds for another use.

Next, pour 1 tablespoon fresh lemon juice into a small bowl and whisk in ¼ teaspoon kosher salt. Whisk in 2 tablespoons extra-virgin olive oil in a thin stream until slightly thickened. Stir in the diced fennel bulb, the minced fennel fronds, 1 seeded and diced tomato, 1 seeded and minced jalapeño chile (or to taste), 1 tablespoon minced fresh basil, and 1 teaspoon minced fresh tarragon.

Just before serving, gently mix the diced salmon into the fennel mixture. Adjust the seasonings and serve.

Salmon Tartare with Soy, Sesame & Wasabi

Serve this Asian-inspired tartare with fluted cucumber slices (page 41) or with Toast Cups (page 22).

Rinse and trim a 9–10 oz (280–315 g) never-frozen, skinned wild salmon fillet. Pull out any pin bones with small tweezers and finely dice the fish.

Pour 1 tablespoon fresh lime juice into a small bowl. Whisk in 2 tablespoons Asian sesame oil in a thin stream until slightly thickened. Put ½ teaspoon wasabi powder in a separate small bowl and stir in 2 teaspoons soy sauce until the powder is dissolved. Whisk the wasabi mixture into the oil mixture. Stir in 1 thinly sliced large green (spring) onion (white and tender green parts), 1½ teaspoons minced fresh ginger, and 1 teaspoon toasted black sesame seeds (page 42).

Just before serving, mix the diced salmon into the wasabi mixture. Gently stir in ⅓ cup (⅓ oz/10 g) watercress leaves. Adjust the seasonings and serve.

Gravlax

The Scandinavians developed this four-day salt-and-sugar cure, which gives the salmon a complex, mildly briny flavor. During the curing process, excess moisture is leached from the salmon, while the flavors of the herbs and spices are absorbed. The flesh also turns an intriguing translucent shade of orange.

1 Rinse the salmon and check for errant bones
Rinse the salmon and pat dry with paper towels. Measure the length of the salmon fillet and cut a piece of waxed paper about 2½ times its length. Lay the salmon on the center of the waxed paper. Run your fingertips along both sides of the fillet to check for any small bones, known as *pin bones*. Using small tweezers or fish pliers, pull out the bones.

2 Mix together the cure mixtures
In a small glass or ceramic bowl, stir together the salt, sugar, and lemon zest. Place the peppercorns and coriander seeds in a spice grinder or an electric coffee grinder reserved only for spices and process until coarsely ground. Add to the salt mixture and mix well. In another bowl, stir together the dill, tarragon, and mint.

3 Rub the salmon with the cure
Evenly drizzle half of the Cognac over the salmon. Then, evenly sprinkle with half of the salt mixture, pressing it into the flesh with your fingers, and half of the herb mixture, again pressing it into the flesh. Turn over the fillet and repeat with the remaining Cognac, salt mixture, and herb mixture, again pressing all of them in well. Wrap the fillet tightly in the waxed paper. Cut a piece of aluminum foil about 2½ times the length of the fillet. Wrap the fillet tightly in the foil.

4 Cure the salmon
Place the salmon in a large cake pan or other rimmed pan. Place a slightly smaller pan on top of the salmon. Place weights, such as heavy canned goods, in the top pan. Refrigerate the weighted salmon for 4 days, turning it over once a day. At the end of the fourth day, unwrap the salmon and rinse it briefly under running cool water to remove most of the curing ingredients. Dry well with paper towels and use now, or wrap well and refrigerate for up to 3 days before serving.

5 Serve the cured salmon
If you have refrigerated the fish, remove it from the refrigerator 15 minutes before serving. Using a long, sharp slicing knife, cut the salmon on the diagonal into paper-thin slices. Arrange them, slightly overlapping, on a platter. Put the cream cheese in a small bowl with a small spreading knife. Put the capers, onion, and dill in separate small serving bowls with small serving spoons. Place the bread in a napkin-lined basket. Let guests assemble their own canapés, spreading the bread with cream cheese, if desired; sprinkling on the capers, onion, and dill; and topping with a piece of salmon. Keep any leftover salmon, well wrapped, in the refrigerator for up to 1 week.

1 piece never-frozen center-cut wild salmon fillet, about 1½ lb (750 g) and of uniform thickness, skinned by the fishmonger

1½ tablespoons kosher salt

1 teaspoon sugar

Finely grated zest of 1 lemon (page 43)

1½ teaspoons peppercorns

1 teaspoon coriander seeds

1 tablespoon coarsely chopped fresh dill (page 42)

1 tablespoon coarsely chopped fresh tarragon (page 42)

1 tablespoon coarsely chopped fresh mint (page 42)

1 tablespoon Cognac

For serving

1 package (8 oz/250 g) cream cheese, at room temperature

⅓ cup (2½ oz/75 g) capers, rinsed and drained

1 small red onion, minced (page 38)

⅓ cup (½ oz/15 g) minced fresh dill (page 42)

16–24 slices cocktail-sized pumpernickel bread or 8–12 miniature bagels, halved

MAKES 4–6 SERVINGS

Oysters on the Half Shell with Mignonette Sauce

Plump, briny oysters need little embellishment. This simple, tart, peppery sauce is the classic accompaniment. Oysters are available year-round, but they are best in the cooler months. In summer, their traditional spawning season, oysters typically have less flavor, a softer texture, and a milky cast.

For the sauce

3 tablespoons fresh lemon juice (page 43)

2 tablespoons sherry vinegar

1 small shallot, minced (page 38)

1 teaspoon coarsely crushed peppercorns

¼ teaspoon kosher salt

2–3 dozen oysters in the shell

Crushed ice

MAKES 4–6 SERVINGS

CHEF'S TIP

Look for crushed ice in bags in freezers at the supermarket or liquor store. Or, make your own: Put ice cubes in a blender and process until crushed. Alternatively, place them in a heavy-duty locking plastic bag and seal it well. Use a rolling pin or meat pounder to break the cubes into small shards.

1 **Make the sauce**
Prepare this sauce at least 2 hours in advance—or preferably the day before—to allow its flavors to blend and mellow. In a small bowl, combine the lemon juice and vinegar. Stir in the shallot, peppercorns, and salt. Cover and set aside at room temperature until serving.

2 **Scrub the oysters**
As soon as you get the oysters home from the fishmonger, scrub the shells with a stiff brush under running cold water to remove any dirt. If any of the oysters are open, tap them lightly on the countertop. Discard any open oysters that do not close (oysters that remain open are dead and could be dangerous to eat). Store the oysters, cupped side down, on a rimmed baking sheet in the refrigerator until ready to serve. Cover with a damp cloth or paper towels to keep them moist.

3 **Shuck the oysters**
Wait until just before serving time to open the oysters. Have ready a large, flat-rimmed serving dish with crushed ice. If you are not sure how to *shuck*, or open, oysters, turn to page 46. Protect your nondominant hand with a folded thick kitchen towel or thick pot holder. Working with 1 oyster at a time, place it flat side up and cupped shell down, on the towel. Locate the hinge between the flat lid and the cupped body at the pointed end of the oyster. Move an oyster knife over the hinge to see where you can get in and insert the tip of the knife into the hinge. Keep pushing the knife steadily into this spot until about ½ inch (12 mm) of the tip disappears inside the oyster. Twist the knife sharply to lift open the top shell, then run the knife along the inside surface of the top shell to detach the muscle that connects the oyster. As you work, be careful not to lose the precious juice, or oyster *liquor*. Bend the top shell backward, snapping it off at the hinge. Discard the top shell. Run the knife along the inside surface of the bottom shell to loosen the oyster completely, then leave the oyster in this half shell. Repeat the *shucking* process with the remaining oysters.

4 **Serve the oysters**
Arrange the oysters on top of the ice on the serving dish. Drizzle a few drops of the sauce on each oyster, or place the sauce in a serving bowl with a small spoon and let guests help themselves. Provide guests with small plates and forks for eating the oysters and a bowl for discarding the empty shells.

Deviled Eggs

The success of this old-fashioned favorite depends on tender egg whites and a creamy filling. Dill, celery, mayonnaise, and mustard, which all add flavor to the rich yolks, are classic additions to the filling, but I've also mixed in peppery arugula and piquant capers to give the recipe a contemporary profile. Make sure all of the ingredients are minced finely enough to pass through the pastry-bag tip.

1 Cook and cool the eggs

Carefully place the eggs in a wide, deep saucepan. Add water to cover by 1 inch (2.5 cm), place over medium heat, and bring to a boil. As soon as you see large bubbles begin to form, remove the pan from the heat, cover, and let stand for about 15 minutes. (If you let the eggs boil, they will be tough and rubbery.) Drain the eggs, return them to the pan, and add cold water to cover. Then fill the pan with ice cubes. Cooling the eggs with ice water will halt the cooking and make the eggs easier to peel. Let the eggs stand until cold to the touch, about 15 minutes.

2 Peel the eggs

Carefully drain the water from the eggs, leaving them in the pan. Shake the pan gently so the eggs collide and crack. One at a time, roll an egg between your hands to loosen and crack the entire shell. Starting from the large end, use your fingertips to peel off the shell. Rinse off any clinging bits of shell and pat the eggs dry with paper towels. (You can prepare eggs up to this point, place in a covered container, and refrigerate for up to 2 days. Remove them 2 hours before filling.)

3 Prepare the filling

Rinse a large, sharp knife under cold water to ensure a clean cut, wipe the knife dry, and then cut an egg in half lengthwise. Repeat with the remaining eggs, rinsing and drying the knife before each cut. Using a small spoon, scoop out the yolk from each half and transfer to a coarse-mesh sieve placed over a bowl. Use the back of the spoon to push the yolks through the sieve. Using a fork, mash the mayonnaise into the yolks. Stir in the capers, arugula, green onion, minced dill, celery, and pepper. Taste and add a pinch of salt if the filling tastes dull—the amount will depend on how salty the mayonnaise is.

4 Assemble a pastry bag and fill the eggs

If you are new to using a pastry (piping) bag, turn to page 30. Fit a pastry bag with a star tip and fill the bag with the egg yolk mixture. Position the tip just above an egg half. Apply gentle pressure to pipe a rosette into the egg cavity. When the hollow is filled, release the pressure, twirl and lift the bag away, and move to the next egg. Repeat until all the halves are filled.

5 Serve the eggs

Transfer the filled eggs to a serving platter and garnish each egg with a dill sprig. Serve within 1 hour of filling.

---

6 extra-large eggs

Ice cubes

¼ cup (2 fl oz/60 ml) mayonnaise

1 tablespoon brine-packed capers, rinsed, drained, and finely minced

1 tablespoon finely minced arugula (rocket)

1 tablespoon finely minced green (spring) onion, white and tender green parts (page 40)

1 tablespoon finely minced fresh dill (page 42)

1 tablespoon finely minced celery

⅛ teaspoon freshly ground pepper

Kosher salt, if needed

12 tiny sprigs fresh dill

MAKES 4–6 SERVINGS

SHORTCUT

You can also use a small spoon and small rubber spatula to fill the eggs. Use the spoon to scoop up the filling, then release the filling cleanly into the egg with the spatula.

Prosciutto-Wrapped Figs & Melon

Here, two sweet, fragrant summer fruits pair perfectly with the rich-tasting salt-cured ham of Italy. Ripe figs are a special treat, and you should take advantage of them when their short season hits in late summer. If they are unavailable, double the amount of cantaloupe, which is at its peak from midsummer to early autumn.

1 ripe cantaloupe

12 small ripe Black Mission figs

8 paper-thin slices imported Italian prosciutto such as *prosciutto di Parma*

24 tiny leaves fresh mint, optional

MAKES 4–6 SERVINGS

CHEF'S TIP

To find a ripe cantaloupe, look for one with a strong, sweet fragrance and that gives slightly when pressed at both ends. Check the end to make sure there is no green stem, ragged fibers, or an irregular scar where the stem once was. Any evidence of a stem indicates the fruit was picked before it was ripe.

1 Prepare the melon

Rinse the melon skin well to rid it of any dirt and impurities. Pat dry with paper towels. Place the melon on a cutting board and, using a chef's knife, halve the melon through the stem end. Using a spoon, scoop out the seeds and any fibers from the center and discard. Save one of the melon halves for another use, and cut the remaining half into narrow slices each 1¼ inches (3 cm) thick. To remove the skin from each slice, slip the knife between the flesh and the skin and carefully cut away the skin. Cut off the curled ends of each slice and save for another use. Cut the melon slices into small pieces, each ¾ inch (2 cm) wide (you should have 12 pieces total). If desired, place the melon pieces in a small bowl, cover with plastic wrap, and refrigerate for up to 4 hours.

2 Prepare the figs

Run the figs under running cold water to rinse them briefly, then pat them dry with paper towels. Keep the stems on the figs, if desired, as a natural handle for guests to use when eating.

3 Prepare the prosciutto

One at a time, lay the prosciutto slices flat on a cutting board. Use a chef's knife to cut each slice lengthwise into 3 pieces.

4 Wrap the melon and figs with prosciutto

As close to serving time as possible, wrap each piece of melon and each fig with a strip of prosciutto. If the prosciutto is moist, it will stick to the fruit without help. If it doesn't stick, place a toothpick through the prosciutto to secure it to the fruit. Tuck a mint leaf, if using, into the prosciutto.

5 Serve the prosciutto-wrapped fruits

Arrange the fruits on a platter, alternating the figs and melon pieces. Alternatively, place the figs in the center of a circular platter and arrange the melon pieces in a ring around them. Serve right away. If you are serving the figs with their stems attached, provide guests with small plates so they have a place to put the stems when they are finished.

Honey-Glazed Spiced Nuts

When using nuts for this or many other dishes, I roast them to a medium brown to intensify their flavor and increase their crunch. The heat also releases their fragrance, which mingles with the bold spices used in the glaze. The honey and lemon juice add sweet and tangy layers to the flavorful glaze as well.

1 **Preheat the oven**
Preheat the oven to 300°F (150°C). Line a rimmed baking sheet with aluminum foil.

2 **Grind the seeds**
Place the cumin seeds and coriander seeds in a spice grinder or an electric coffee grinder reserved only for spices. Process the seeds until finely ground and pour into a small bowl. (Alternatively, grind the seeds in a mortar with a pestle.)

3 **Make the glaze**
In a heavy-bottomed saucepan, combine the butter, honey, lemon juice, chipotle powder, ground cumin and coriander seeds, salt, and cayenne. Place over medium-low heat and cook, stirring constantly with a heatproof silicone spatula, until the butter and honey have melted and all the ingredients are well combined.

4 **Add the nuts**
Raise the heat to medium-high and immediately stir in all the nuts. Continue stirring with the spatula until the nuts are evenly coated and any liquid is absorbed, about 2 minutes.

5 **Adjust the seasonings**
Taste the coated nuts. If you want a spicier mix, add more cayenne. If you prefer the nuts to taste tangier, add more lemon juice. In general, you want the flavors to be balanced and unified; no one ingredient or flavor (such as sweetness or spiciness) should be more pronounced than another.

6 **Roast and serve the nuts**
Transfer the coated nuts to the prepared baking sheet, spreading them in a single layer. Using 2 knives, separate any nuts that are stuck together. Roast the nuts, stirring them occasionally with a silicone spatula, until they are shiny and turn a rich medium brown, about 30 minutes. Watch the nuts carefully to be sure they don't overbrown. Remove the baking sheet from the oven and use the knives to separate any nuts that are stuck together. Let the nuts cool on the baking sheet for at least 15 minutes. Transfer the cooled nuts to a bowl and serve.

For the glaze

1 teaspoon cumin seeds

1 teaspoon coriander seeds

2 tablespoons unsalted butter

2 tablespoons honey

½ teaspoon fresh lemon juice (page 43)

1 teaspoon chipotle or other chile powder

⅛ teaspoon kosher salt

⅛ teaspoon cayenne pepper

1¾ cups (8 oz/250 g) raw almonds, cashews, pecans, or walnuts, or a combination

MAKES 4–6 SERVINGS

MAKE-AHEAD TIP
You can arrange the nuts on the baking sheet and set aside at room temperature for up to 6 hours before you plan to roast them. Or, you can roast the nuts a day in advance and store them, covered in the serving bowl, at room temperature. If you prefer to serve them warm, leave them on the baking sheet and place in a preheated 350°F (180°C) oven for 3–4 minutes.

5

Hot Hors d'Oeuvres

Once you've mastered the recipes in this chapter, you'll have some crowning achievements to add to your growing repertory of hors d'oeuvres. Tartlets, turnovers, filo triangles, and gougères are always crowd-pleasers, but keep in mind they take some practice and patience for the home cook. Try simpler skewers, bruschetta, and stuffed clams when you're pressed for time.

Chicken Skewers with Peanut Dipping Sauce

The peanut dipping sauce that accompanies these chicken skewers is rich, creamy, and packed with the tart, hot, and spicy flavors of Asia. The tender but naturally mild chicken spends time in a marinade that carries the same bold and complex seasoning.

1 Prepare the chicken breasts

Rinse the chicken and pat dry with paper towels. Using a chef's knife, cut the tenderloin (the strip of meat, or muscle, that attaches the breast to the breastbone) from each breast half and reserve for another use. Trim off any fat and membrane from the breasts. One at a time, place the chicken breast halves between 2 pieces of waxed paper, positioning the breast vertically and with the thinner tapered part closest to you. Using a meat pounder, gently pound the thicker top of the breast half out and away from you until the meat is equally thick throughout. Slice each breast half lengthwise into strips 1 inch (2.5 cm) wide. Slice the strips crosswise into 1-inch square pieces. You should have about 9 pieces from each breast half. Place the pieces in a shallow ceramic or glass dish. Keep any leftover thin ends and triangular pieces and reserve them, with the tenderloins, for another use.

2 Soak the skewers

Place 27 wooden skewers (1 skewer for each piece of chicken) in a long, shallow dish and cover with water. Let them soak in the refrigerator for at least 1 hour. Soaking and chilling the skewers will prevent them from scorching.

3 Prepare the ginger and jalapeño chile

If you are new to working with ginger and chiles, turn to pages 44 and 45. First, dice the ginger: Using a vegetable peeler, remove the thin skin from the ginger. Slice about ½ inch (12 mm) of the knob into disks about ⅛ inch (3 mm) thick and then slice the disks into strips about ⅛ inch wide. Cut the strips crosswise into ⅛-inch dice. Measure out 2 teaspoons diced ginger. Then, dice the jalapeño chile: With a small, sharp knife, cut the chile lengthwise into quarters. With the tip of the knife, cut the stem, ribs, and seeds from each quarter. Slice each quarter into narrow strips about ⅛ inch thick. Cut the strips crosswise into ⅛-inch dice. >

3 large boneless, skinless chicken breast halves, 7–8 oz (220–250 g) each

For the marinade and dipping sauce

1 small knob fresh ginger

1 jalapeño chile, or more if desired for a hotter dipping sauce

3 tablespoons peanut oil, plus more for preparing the pan

3 tablespoons Asian sesame oil

2 tablespoons unseasoned rice vinegar

1 tablespoon fresh lime juice

3 large cloves garlic, halved

3 tablespoons coarsely chopped fresh mint

⅓ cup (3½ oz/105 g) natural-style smooth peanut butter

1 tablespoon soy sauce

About ¼ teaspoon kosher salt, optional

For serving

⅛ teaspoon kosher salt

1 green (spring) onion, white and tender green parts, thinly sliced (page 40)

MAKES 6 SERVINGS

4 Make the marinade

Measure the peanut and sesame oils into a glass measuring cup. In a blender, combine the vinegar, lime juice, garlic, ginger, half of the chile, and the mint. Blend on high speed until a smooth purée forms with only fine flecks of green. Stop the blender occasionally to scrape down the sides with a rubber spatula. With the blender running, add the oils, a little at a time, through the feed hole in the lid, pouring them in a thin stream. As you add the oils, check the mixture from time to time. If droplets of oil remain on the surface, run the machine until they are incorporated before adding additional oil. (The marinade can be made up to 8 hours in advance of using, covered, and kept at room temperature.)

5 Marinate the chicken

Drizzle 3 tablespoons of the marinade over the chicken, and toss the chicken until it is evenly coated. Cover and let marinate in the refrigerator, turning occasionally, for about 2 hours. Leave the remaining marinade in the blender for making the dipping sauce.

6 Make the dipping sauce

Add the peanut butter and soy sauce to the blender with the remaining marinade. Blend on high speed until all the ingredients are well mixed.

CHEF'S TIP
When measuring sticky ingredients such as peanut butter, first lightly coat the measuring cup with oil so the ingredient will slip out easily and cleanly.

7 Adjust the seasonings

Taste the dipping sauce and add the salt if the soy sauce has not made the mixture salty enough. Then taste the sauce again. If it is not tangy enough, add more lime juice or vinegar. If it is not spicy enough, add more chile. If it needs more zip, add more ginger or mint. Add any of the ingredients a little at a time and blend briefly until you are happy with the flavor balance. Transfer the sauce to a small serving bowl. Set aside until serving. ›

8 Ready the equipment for broiling

About 20 minutes before you plan to cook the chicken, remove it from the refrigerator and let it come to room temperature. Place an oven rack as close to the heat source as possible and preheat the broiler (grill). Line the bottom of a broiler pan or a rimmed baking sheet with aluminum foil. Cover the broiler pan with its perforated top, or place a cooling rack on top of the baking sheet. Brush the pan top or rack with peanut oil. Have ready 1 baking sheet to hold the uncooked skewers and another to hold the cooked skewers.

CHEF'S TIP

You can also grill these skewers. Prepare a medium-hot fire for direct grilling in a charcoal grill, or preheat a gas grill to medium-high. Grill the skewers, turning once after about 1 ½ minutes, until the chicken is just firm to the touch, opaque throughout, and browned on both sides, 3–4 minutes total.

9 Skewer the chicken

Drain the skewers. Thread 1 piece of chicken onto each skewer, poking the skewer lengthwise through the center of each piece so the skewers can lie flat. Arrange the uncooked skewers on one of the baking sheets.

10 Broil the skewers

Arrange as many skewers as will fit on the broiler pan or cooling rack without touching. Slide the pan under the broiler and broil (grill), turning once after about 2 minutes, until the chicken is just firm to the touch and opaque throughout, about 4 minutes total. To check for doneness, press against the meat with a fingertip. If it feels soft, it is underdone; continue to cook for 1–2 minutes longer. If it is just firm to the touch, remove a skewer from the pan and cut into the chicken with a sharp knife to check that it is opaque. When the chicken is ready, transfer the skewers to the second baking sheet. Cover loosely with aluminum foil to keep warm while you broil the remaining skewers.

11 Serve the skewers

Let the chicken rest for 5–10 minutes to allow the juices to redistribute evenly throughout the meat. Lightly season both sides of the chicken with the salt. Garnish the dipping sauce with the green onion, and place the bowl on a large serving platter. Arrange the skewers next to the bowl and serve right away. Be sure to set out a receptacle for discarding the used skewers.

Serving ideas

A bite of succulent chicken on a skewer is irresistible on its own, but you can dress it up, too. Add a second ingredient, such as green onion, for color and flavor. You can also serve the skewers and dipping sauce in a single package by putting a dab of sauce and then a tiny garnish on the chicken. For more substantial skewers reminiscent of Southeast Asian satay, thread strips of meat, rather than cubes, onto the skewers.

Green onions (top left)
Including a second ingredient on a skewer adds color and flavor. Choose a vegetable that complements your sauce. Green (spring) onions (shown here) or cherry tomatoes are both good choices.

Peanut sauce as a garnish (left)
For a more elegant presentation, apply the sauce directly to the skewers as a garnish and eliminate the need to dip.

Chicken strips (above)
Thread 3-by-1-inch (7.5-by-2.5-cm) strips of chicken breast onto the skewers to make satay. You can use this same technique with beef or pork strips, too. All will taste delicious with the peanut dipping sauce.

Skewer Variations

When entertaining, you'll find that skewers are often the first hors d'oeuvre people pick up. It's difficult to resist a bite of golden brown chicken or other delicious offering, especially with a dipping sauce nearby. After broiling the chicken skewers on page 99, try applying the same technique to other ingredients, including shrimp, beef, lamb, and pork. It even works with sturdy vegetables and fruits. As in the original recipe, most of the variations below call for marinades that can later be used as the base for a dipping sauce, which means that these hors d'oeuvres are also deceptively simple to make. Each variation makes 6 servings.

Shrimp Skewers with Asian Pesto Sauce

This Asian-inspired marinade and dipping sauce is perfect with shrimp.

Peel and devein 1 lb (500 g) large shrimp (prawns) and put in a glass bowl. Soak 25–30 skewers.

Make the marinade: In a blender, purée 3 tablespoons reduced-sodium soy sauce, 2 tablespoons fresh lemon juice, 1 tablespoon balsamic vinegar, 1 tablespoon finely diced fresh ginger, 2 halved large garlic cloves, and ½ cup (4 fl oz/125 ml) extra-virgin olive oil. Drizzle 3 tablespoons over the shrimp.

Make the dipping sauce: Add 2 tablespoons toasted pine nuts (page 42), 1 minced jalapeño chile (or to taste), ¼ cup (⅓ oz/ 10 g) coarsely chopped fresh basil, and 1 tablespoon coarsely chopped fresh mint to the marinade in the blender and purée until smooth. Adjust the seasonings, adding ¼ teaspoon kosher salt if needed.

Thread each shrimp onto a soaked skewer, passing it through the body twice, near the head and the tail. Broil (grill), turning once after 2 minutes, until pink and firm, 3–4 minutes total. Serve with the dipping sauce.

Beef Skewers with Mustard Dipping Sauce

This zesty mustard sauce serves as both a marinade and a dipping sauce.

Cut 1½ lb (750 g) beef filet or London broil into 1-inch (2.5-cm) cubes and put in a glass dish. Soak 18–27 skewers.

Make the marinade: In a small bowl, whisk together ¼ cup (2 oz/60 g) Dijon mustard, 2 tablespoons fresh lemon juice, and 1 tablespoon soy sauce. Gradually whisk in ½ cup (4 fl oz/125 ml) extra-virgin olive oil until the mixture thickens. Stir in 1 thinly sliced large green (spring) onion (white and tender green parts), 1 minced large garlic clove, 1 tablespoon minced fresh rosemary, and ¼ teaspoon freshly ground pepper. Drizzle 2 tablespoons over the beef.

Make the dipping sauce: Stir 2 teaspoons rinsed and dried brine-packed green peppercorns into the remaining marinade. Adjust the seasonings.

Thread the beef cubes onto the soaked skewers. Broil (grill), turning once after 2–3 minutes, until lightly browned and medium-rare, 4–6 minutes total. Lightly season all sides of the beef with ¼ teaspoon kosher salt. Serve with the dipping sauce.

Lamb Skewers with Yogurt Dipping Sauce

The traditional Mediterranean flavors in this marinade and dipping sauce are a customary match with lamb.

Cut 1½ lb (750 g) lamb sirloin into 1-inch (2.5-cm) cubes and put in a glass dish. Soak 18–27 skewers.

Make the marinade: In a small bowl, whisk together ¼ cup (2 fl oz/60 ml) extra-virgin olive oil, 2 teaspoons fresh lemon juice, 2 minced large garlic cloves, 1 teaspoon ground cumin, 3 tablespoons minced fresh dill, and ¼ teaspoon freshly ground pepper. Reserve 3 tablespoons of the marinade, then drizzle the rest over the lamb.

Make the dipping sauce: Stir the reserved marinade into 1 cup (8 oz/250 g) plain yogurt along with 1 tablespoon minced fresh mint and ⅛ teaspoon freshly ground white pepper. Adjust the seasonings.

Thread the lamb cubes onto the soaked skewers. Broil (grill), turning once after 2–3 minutes, until lightly browned and medium-rare, 4–6 minutes total. Lightly season all sides of the lamb with ¼ teaspoon kosher salt. Serve with the dipping sauce.

Pork Skewers with Fruit Dipping Sauce

Pork pairs well with fruit, such as the tart pomegranate sauce in this recipe.

Cut 1¼ lb (625 g) pork tenderloin into 1-inch (2.5-cm) cubes and put in a glass dish. Soak 18–27 skewers.

Make the marinade: In a bowl, whisk together 1 teaspoon finely grated orange zest, 3 tablespoons fresh orange juice, and 2 tablespoons sherry vinegar. Gradually whisk in 6 tablespoons (3 fl oz/90 ml) extra-virgin olive oil until the mixture thickens. Whisk in 1 tablespoon pomegranate molasses, 1 minced small garlic clove, ½ teaspoon finely ground aniseeds, and ½ teaspoon freshly ground coarse pepper. Drizzle ¼ cup (2 fl oz/ 60 ml) of the marinade over the pork. Cover and let stand at room temperature for 30 minutes.

Make the dipping sauce: Whisk 3 tablespoons pomegranate molasses and 1 thinly sliced green (spring) onion (white and tender green parts) into the remaining marinade. Adjust the seasonings, adding ¼ teaspoon kosher salt if needed.

Thread the pork cubes onto the soaked skewers. Broil (grill), turning once after 3 minutes, until lightly browned, firm, and slightly pink in the center, about 5 minutes total. Lightly season all sides of the pork with ¼ teaspoon kosher salt.

Just before serving, whisk 1 teaspoon finely grated orange zest into the dipping sauce and serve with the skewers.

Vegetable Skewers with Anchovy Dipping Sauce

This warm sauce, similar to Italian *bagna cauda,* is terrific with broiled vegetables.

Trim the stems of 25–30 white button mushrooms even with the caps. Cut 2 trimmed zucchini (courgettes) crosswise into ¾-inch (2-cm) pieces. Cut 2 large stemmed and seeded red bell peppers (capsicums) into 1½-inch (4-cm) squares. Soak about 40 skewers.

Make the marinade: In a small saucepan over medium-low heat, combine ⅓ cup (3 fl oz/80 ml) extra-virgin olive oil and 6 tablespoons (3 oz/90 g) unsalted butter. When the butter has melted, add 3 minced garlic cloves and cook until the garlic is soft but not brown, 3–4 minutes. Let cool.

Thread the zucchini like a lollipop through the center and the mushrooms vertically through the stem onto the soaked skewers. Add 1 square of bell pepper to each skewer and brush on both sides with some of the marinade.

Make the dipping sauce: Add 3 minced olive oil–packed anchovy fillets and ⅛ teaspoon red pepper flakes to the pan with the remaining marinade. Warm over very low heat until the anchovies have been incorporated, 3–4 minutes. Set aside and keep warm.

Broil (grill) the vegetables, turning once after 5 minutes, until lightly browned, 8–9 minutes total. Lightly season all sides of the vegetables with ¼ teaspoon kosher salt. Pour the warm dipping sauce into a heatproof bowl and serve with the skewers.

Fruit Skewers with Honey-Yogurt Dipping Sauce

Skewers of pineapple chunks and whole strawberries are unique sweet hors d'oeuvres.

Cut off the top (crown) and bottom from 1 medium-ripe pineapple, about 4 lb (2 kg). Holding the pineapple upright, slice off the skin in long strips, leaving the small brown "eyes." Lay the pineapple on its side. Align the knife blade with the diagonal rows of eyes and cut shallow furrows, following a spiral pattern, to remove all the eyes. Cut the pineapple crosswise into slices ¾ inch (2 cm) thick. Use a small knife to cut out the tough center core from each slice and discard. Cut the rings into eighths to create chunks. Hull and rinse 2 baskets (about 12 oz/375 g each) large straw-berries and pat dry with paper towels. Soak about 40 skewers.

Make the dipping sauce: In a small bowl, whisk together 1 cup (8 oz/250 g) plain yogurt, 2 teaspoons finely grated orange zest, 2 tablespoons fresh orange juice, 2 tablespoons honey, and ¼ teaspoon kosher salt. Pour into a serving bowl.

Thread the pineapple chunks lengthwise through the center and the strawberries through the stem end onto the soaked skewers. Lightly brush the fruit with 2 teaspoons soybean oil and season with ½ teaspoon freshly ground pepper. Broil (grill), turning once after 2 minutes, just until warmed through, about 4 minutes total. Serve with the dipping sauce.

Bacon & Onion Tartlets

These tartlets, which call for a tender, flaky pastry dough, are filled with a custard base made from cream and eggs and seasoned with crisp bacon and caramelized onions. I like to use small boat-shaped fluted molds for the tartlets, as they add instant elegance to the presentation.

1 Make the dough

If you need help making tartlet dough, turn to page 18. Fit a food processor with the metal blade and add the flours and salt. Pulse to combine the ingredients. Add the butter and process with on-off pulses until the butter has flattened into flakes and the rest of the mixture looks like grated Parmesan cheese, about 5 seconds. Using a rubber spatula, scrape down the sides of the work bowl. With the processor running, quickly pour the egg through the feed tube and process with on-off pulses just until the mixture comes together in clumps; do not allow it to form a ball. (If you process the dough beyond this point, it will toughen.) Turn the dough out onto a lightly floured work surface. Using both hands and a bench scraper, gently push the dough together into a single mass and shape it into a rectangle about 6 by 3½ inches (15 by 9 cm). Place the dough in a locking plastic bag and refrigerate it for at least 2 hours or up to 2 days.

2 Prepare the barquette molds

Using a pastry brush, coat sixteen 4½-inch (11.5-cm) fluted barquette molds with the melted butter. Arrange 12 of the molds as close together as possible in 3 rows on a flat work surface, placing each mold in the second row between 2 molds in the first row, to form a large rectangle. Set the other 4 molds aside. Measure the space the molds occupy on the work surface and note the measurement.

3 Roll out the dough

If you are new to rolling out pastry dough, turn to page 31. Tear off 2 sheets of waxed paper, each about 15 inches (38 cm) long. Remove the dough from the bag, place it between the sheets on a work surface, and whack it several times with a heavy rolling pin to soften it. Roll out the dough lengthwise and crosswise, alternating directions and turning the dough over from time to time, into a rectangle that measures the same size as the space the molds occupy. The dough should be about ⅛ inch (3 mm) thick. If the dough looks wrinkled, lift off the waxed paper and smooth it again over the dough. If the dough becomes too soft at any point, refrigerate it for about 15 minutes to firm it. ›

For the tartlet dough

1 cup (5 oz/155 g) unbleached all-purpose (plain) flour

¼ cup (1 oz/30 g) cake (soft-wheat) flour

½ teaspoon kosher salt

½ cup (4 oz/125 g) cold unsalted butter, cut into 1-inch (2.5-cm) pieces

1 cold large egg, lightly beaten with a fork

1 tablespoon unsalted butter, melted, for preparing the molds

For the filling and topping

3 slices bacon or pancetta, about 2½ oz (75 g) total weight

4 large yellow or red onions, about 2 lb (1 kg) total weight

1 tablespoon extra-virgin olive oil

5 sprigs fresh thyme

⅔ cup (5 fl oz/160 ml) heavy (double) cream

2 large eggs

½ teaspoon kosher salt

⅛ teaspoon freshly ground pepper

⅛ teaspoon freshly grated nutmeg (page 43)

14 blades fresh chives

1 tablespoon freshly grated Parmigiano-Reggiano cheese

MAKES 16 TARTLETS, OR 4–8 SERVINGS

CHEF'S TIP
When grinding small amounts of pepper, you can estimate the amount by counting the number of turns of the pepper mill: 10 turns equals about ⅛ teaspoon.

4
⌄⌄

5

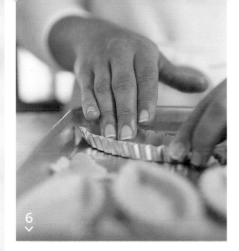

4 Line the tartlet molds with the dough

Peel off the top piece of waxed paper, then carefully flip the dough over the 12 molds, bottom paper side up. Make sure all the molds are covered by the pastry. Press the dough onto the molds through the paper, and then peel off the paper.

5 Trim the dough

Run the rolling pin across the top of the molds, pressing firmly on the edges to trim the dough from the molds. Separate the molds, remove the dough trimmings, and reserve. Reroll the dough trimmings into a rectangle, divide it into 4 pieces, and pat into the remaining 4 molds, trimming as necessary.

6 Dock and chill the dough

Using your fingers, gently push the dough down into the bottom and up the sides of the molds to the rim, pressing down so the dough adheres. Place the tartlet molds on a large rimmed baking sheet. Prick the dough all over with the tines of a fork so it doesn't puff up during baking; this technique is known as *docking*. Cover the molds with waxed paper and freeze for at least 30 minutes or refrigerate for at least 2 hours or up to 3 days. Chilling the dough-lined molds will help prevent the dough from shrinking when you bake it, and it will help the dough keep its shape.

7 Blind bake the tartlet shells

Position a rack in the middle of the oven and preheat the oven to 375°F (190°C). Cut out sixteen 5-by-6-inch (13-by-15-cm) rectangles of aluminum foil. Gently press a piece of foil over the bottom and up the sides of each mold. Fold the foil down around the molds and fill the lined molds with pie weights or dried beans. Bake the molds for 10 minutes, then rotate the sheet 180 degrees and bake about 5 minutes longer. (Changing the position of the sheet prevents uneven browning.) Remove the sheet with the molds and carefully remove the weights and foil from each mold. Return the sheet with the uncovered tartlet shells to the oven and bake until the bottom of the pastry is dry, 1–2 minutes longer. Remove the sheet from the oven and let cool on a wire rack for at least 10 minutes while you make the filling.

8 Dice the bacon and onions

If you need help dicing the bacon or onions, turn to pages 45 and 38. First dice the bacon: Stack the bacon slices on top of one another on the cutting board and use a chef's knife to slice them lengthwise into narrow strips about ¼ inch (6 mm) wide. Slice the strips crosswise to create ¼-inch dice. Then, dice the onions: Cut the onions in half lengthwise and peel each half. One at a time, place the onion halves, cut side down, on the cutting board. Alternately make a series of lengthwise cuts, parallel cuts, then crosswise cuts to create ¼-inch dice. Be sure to stop just short of the root end; this holds the onion half together as you cut.

9 Cook the bacon

Line a large plate with a paper towel. Place a heavy frying pan over medium heat and add the olive oil. When the surface just shimmers, add the bacon and cook, stirring occasionally, until brown and crisp, about 3 minutes. Remove from the heat and, using a slotted spoon, transfer the bacon to the paper-lined plate. Top with another paper towel and blot the grease from the top of the bacon.

10 Caramelize the onions

Return the pan to medium-low heat and stir the onions and thyme sprigs into the oil. Cover and cook, stirring occasionally, for 30 minutes. Uncover and cook, watching carefully and stirring frequently toward the end of cooking, until the natural sugars in the onions have caramelized, turning the onions a deep mahogany brown, 20–25 minutes longer. Remove from the heat and transfer to a large bowl to let cool. After the onions have cooled for about 15 minutes, remove and discard the thyme sprigs and stir in the bacon.

11 Mix the filling

In a bowl, combine the cream, eggs, salt, pepper, and nutmeg. Using a whisk, beat the mixture lightly to blend the ingredients. Stir the cream mixture into the cooled onion mixture until well blended.

12 Snip the chives

Using kitchen scissors, snip the chive blades into tiny pieces. (It's best to use scissors rather than a knife for this task; a knife can smash the chives.) Measure out 2 teaspoons snipped chives.

13 Fill the shells and bake the tartlets

Preheat the oven to 400°F (200°C). Use a soupspoon to fill the shells generously with the filling. Sprinkle with the chives and cheese. Bake the tartlets until the filling is puffed, browned, and set, 20–25 minutes. Halfway through baking, rotate the baking sheet 180 degrees to ensure even browning. Remove the baking sheet with the tartlets from the oven and, wearing an oven mitt, carefully pick up and transfer the tartlets to a wire rack to cool for at least 10 minutes. This cooling period will allow the flavors of the tartlets to emerge and make the tartlets easier to unmold.

14 Serve the tartlets

When the tartlets are cool enough to touch, use the tip of a paring knife to ease each tartlet out of its shell, then transfer the tartlets to a serving platter.

Serving ideas

Tartlets can be formed into a variety of shapes and sizes, making them a particularly versatile hors d'oeuvre. Small, round tartlets are probably the most classic shape; both fluted and plain styles are common. Using miniature muffin-tin cups is a great idea if you are making tartlets for a crowd. You can also make a single large rectangular tart and then cut it into narrow wedges or small squares for serving.

Round tartlets (top left)

Use 2½–2¾-inch (6–7-cm) plain or fluted round tartlet pans. The pans will hold about the same amount of dough and filling as the barquette molds.

Muffin cups (left)

Use miniature muffin cups instead of molds to make tartlets quickly. Cut the dough into 3-inch (7.5-cm) rounds and line the muffin cups. Prick the dough with a fork and refrigerate it, but don't blind bake the shells. This method will yield 30 tartlets.

Rectangular tart (above)

Use a rectangular 13¾-by-4¼-inch (35-by-11-cm) tart pan, bake the tart as directed for the barquette molds, and slice into narrow wedges to serve.

Tartlet Variations

The most difficult part about making tartlets is rolling the pastry and fitting it into the molds. Happily, this step will become easier with practice, and the crisp, buttery results are well worth the time and care it takes to get the pastry just right. Once you've mastered making the dough and lining the molds, you can easily vary the fillings. Bacon and caramelized onions are just some of many ingredients you can mix into the custard base. Each of the recipes below adds at least two flavorful ingredients to the custard and often includes a pinch of freshly grated nutmeg—a classic seasoning in many savory egg-and-cream-based dishes. Each variation makes 16 tartlets, or 4 to 8 servings.

Prosciutto & Goat Cheese Tartlets

Salty prosciutto and tangy goat cheese stand in for the bacon and onions in these rustic tartlets.

Follow the recipe for Bacon & Onion Tartlets to make 1 batch Tartlet Dough, roll it out, and blind bake the tartlet shells. Remove the shells from the oven and increase the heat to 400°F (200°C).

Make the filling: In a blender or food processor, combine 6 oz (185 g) fresh goat cheese, preferably Montrachet, and ⅓ cup (3 fl oz/80 ml) heavy (double) cream. Process until well mixed, using brief pulses and stopping occasionally to scrape down the sides of the container. Add ¼ teaspoon freshly ground pepper and ⅛ teaspoon freshly grated nutmeg and process to mix. Taste and adjust the seasonings. Add 2 large eggs and blend completely.

Spoon the filling into the tartlet shells, then divide ¼ cup (1 oz/30 g) minced prosciutto (about 3 thin slices) and 2 teaspoons snipped fresh chives evenly among the tartlets, gently poking them down into the filling. Bake until the filling is puffed, browned, and set, 20–25 minutes. Let cool for 10 minutes, then unmold and serve.

Smoked Salmon & Dill Tartlets

A creamy custard is an ideal way to feature the traditional flavor pairing of smoked salmon and fresh dill.

Follow the recipe for Bacon & Onion Tartlets to make 1 batch Tartlet Dough, roll it out, and blind bake the tartlet shells. Remove the shells from the oven and increase the heat to 400°F (200°C).

Make the filling: In a bowl, combine ¼ lb (125 g) room-temperature cream cheese, ½ cup (4 fl oz/125 ml) heavy (double) cream, ½ teaspoon fresh lemon juice, and 2 large eggs. Whisk until well blended. Use a rubber spatula to gently mix in ½ lb (250 g) diced smoked salmon, 2 tablespoons minced fresh dill, and 1 tablespoon snipped fresh chives until evenly incorporated.

Spoon the filling into the tartlet shells. Bake until the filling is puffed, browned, and set, 20–25 minutes. Let cool for 10 minutes, then unmold and serve.

Leek & Ricotta Tartlets

Fresh herbs and nutmeg flavor these tartlets, which also feature mild leeks and creamy ricotta.

Follow the recipe for Bacon & Onion Tartlets to make 1 batch Tartlet Dough, roll it out, and blind bake the tartlet shells. Remove the shells from the oven and increase the heat to 400°F (200°C).

Make the filling: In a nonstick frying pan over medium-low heat, warm 2 tablespoons olive oil. Add 1 thinly sliced leek (white and pale green parts). Cover and cook, stirring occasionally, until tender, 10–15 minutes. Let cool until warm, about 15 minutes. Transfer the leeks to a bowl. Using a fork, mix in 1 cup (8 oz/250 g) whole-milk ricotta cheese, 2 tablespoons freshly grated *pecorino romano* cheese, and 1 tablespoon coarsely chopped fresh tarragon until blended. Stir in ¼ cup (2 fl oz/60 ml) heavy (double) cream, ½ teaspoon kosher salt, 1 teaspoon freshly ground pepper, and ⅛ teaspoon freshly grated nutmeg. Add 2 large eggs and mix until blended.

Spoon the filling into the tartlet shells. Bake until the filling is puffed, browned, and set, 20–25 minutes. Let cool for 10 minutes, then unmold and serve.

Spinach & Pepper Tartlets

These pretty tartlets feature a trio of favorite Italian ingredients: spinach, roasted peppers, and Fontina cheese.

Follow the recipe for Bacon & Onion Tartlets to make 1 batch Tartlet Dough, roll it out, and blind bake the tartlet shells. Remove the shells from the oven and increase the heat to 400°F (200°C).

Make the filling: Place 1 lb (500 g) stemmed spinach (with the rinsing water still clinging to the leaves) in a large, deep nonreactive pot over medium-high heat and cook, stirring continually, until the leaves are wilted. Cover, reduce the heat to medium-low, and cook, stirring occasionally, until the leaves are tender, about 5 minutes. Drain and rinse the spinach with cold water to stop the cooking. Squeeze out the excess water and chop finely.

In a food processor, process ½ cup (2 oz/60 g) diced Italian Fontina cheese, using brief pulses and stopping to scrape down the sides as needed, until finely chopped. Add 1 roasted and coarsely chopped large red bell pepper (capsicum) (page 44), ¼ cup (2 fl oz/60 ml) heavy (double) cream, ¾ teaspoon kosher salt, ¼ teaspoon freshly ground pepper, and ⅛ teaspoon freshly grated nutmeg. Process, using brief pulses, until finely puréed. Adjust the seasonings. Add 2 large eggs and process until the mixture is well mixed, 3–5 minutes. Transfer to a bowl and stir in the chopped spinach.

Spoon the filling into the tartlet shells. Bake until the filling is puffed, browned, and set, 20–25 minutes. Let cool for 10 minutes, then unmold and serve.

Mushroom Tartlets

Here, fresh mushrooms, shallots, and thyme pair with nutty Gruyère cheese.

Follow the recipe for Bacon & Onion Tartlets to make 1 batch Tartlet Dough, roll it out, and blind bake the tartlet shells. Remove the shells from the oven and increase the heat to 400°F (200°C).

Make the filling: In a large, nonreactive frying pan over medium heat, warm 1½ tablespoons olive oil. Add 1 minced large shallot and sauté until softened, 2–3 minutes. Raise the heat to medium-high, add ⅔ lb (10 oz/315 g) chopped fresh shiitake mushrooms, and sauté until the mushrooms are brown, about 5 minutes. Stir in 2 teaspoons fresh lemon juice, ⅓ cup (5 fl oz/160 ml) low-sodium beef stock, 1 minced large garlic clove, and 5 sprigs fresh thyme. Cook, stirring occasionally, until all the liquid is absorbed, about 30 minutes. Add ⅛ teaspoon *each* freshly ground pepper and freshly grated nutmeg. Adjust the seasonings, adding ¼ teaspoon kosher salt if needed. Let cool until warm, about 15 minutes. Remove and discard the thyme sprigs. In a bowl, use a fork to mix 3 tablespoons heavy (double) cream, 2 large eggs, 3 tablespoons shredded Gruyère cheese, and 3 tablespoons freshly grated Parmigiano-Reggiano cheese. Stir into the mushroom mixture until well blended.

Spoon the filling into the tartlet shells, then sprinkle with 1 tablespoon freshly grated Parmigiano-Reggiano cheese. Bake until the filling is puffed, browned, and set, 20–25 minutes. Let cool for 10 minutes, then unmold and serve.

Tomato, Basil & Mozzarella Tartlets

Typical Italian ingredients shine in this tartlet filling, too.

Follow the recipe for Bacon & Onion Tartlets to make 1 batch Tartlet Dough, roll it out, and blind bake the tartlet shells. Remove the shells from the oven and increase the heat to 400°F (200°C).

Make the filling: In a frying pan over medium heat, warm 2 tablespoons olive oil. Add ⅓ cup (1½ oz/45 g) finely diced yellow onion and sauté until softened, 6–7 minutes. Add 2 minced large garlic cloves and ⅛ teaspoon red pepper flakes and sauté until fragrant, 1–2 minutes. Add 3 seeded and diced tomatoes (about 1 lb/500 g) and ¼ teaspoon kosher salt, raise the heat to medium-high, and cook until almost all the liquid has evaporated, about 10 minutes. Let cool until warm, about 15 minutes. In a bowl, lightly beat 2 large eggs with a fork. Add ½ cup (3 oz/90 g) shredded fresh whole-milk mozzarella cheese, ¼ cup (⅓ oz/10 g) finely chopped fresh basil, and ½ teaspoon kosher salt, mixing well. Stir in the tomato mixture.

Spoon the filling into the tartlet shells. Bake until the filling is puffed, browned, and set, 20–25 minutes. Let cool for 10 minutes, then unmold and serve.

Filo Triangles with Spinach & Feta

Small parcels of paper-thin filo pastry concealing a filling of spinach and feta cheese are known as *spanakópittes* in Greece. The parcels can take many forms, from triangles to beggar's purses, but if made properly, the pastry is always crisp, flaky, and golden when it emerges from the hot oven.

1 Thaw the filo dough (if frozen)
The day before you plan to make the recipe, put the frozen filo, still in its package, in the refrigerator overnight to thaw. Thawing the dough gradually in the refrigerator will keep it from drying out and cracking.

2 Prepare the spinach for the filling
Sort through the spinach, discarding any yellowed or wilted leaves. If your spinach leaves have tough stems, gently fold each of the leaves in half along the stem, with the vein side facing out. Grasp the stem with your other hand and quickly tear it away to remove the coarse, tough part of the vein. Spinach can be very gritty so it is important to rinse it thoroughly. Fill a large bowl with cool water and add the spinach leaves. Swish the leaves around in the water, then lift them out, refill the bowl with water, and dunk the leaves again. Repeat until no grit remains in the bottom of the bowl. Shake the spinach lightly and place it in a large colander to drain. Don't let the spinach get too dry; you want some of the rinsing water to be clinging to the leaves when you cook them.

3 Cook the spinach
Place a large, deep nonreactive pot over medium-high heat. Gradually add the spinach to the pot, stirring it continually until it is completely wilted. (If all the spinach won't fit in the pot, stir the first batch until it is wilted, and then stir in additional spinach as it can be accommodated.) Cover the pot, reduce the heat to medium-low, and cook, stirring occasionally, until all the leaves are tender, about 5 minutes. Place the colander in the sink and transfer the wilted spinach to the colander to drain. Rinse the spinach with cool water to halt the cooking.

4 Cook the onions and garlic
Return the pot to medium heat, allow the liquid to evaporate, then add the olive oil. Reduce the heat to medium-low and add the green onions and garlic. Cook, stirring constantly, just until aromatic, 1–2 minutes. Transfer to a bowl and add the pine nuts, if using.

5 Finish the filling
Crumble the cheese and add it to the onion mixture. Stir in the raisins (if using), parsley, and dill. Add the pepper and nutmeg and mix well. When the spinach is cool, squeeze it over a bowl or the sink to eliminate as much water as possible. Use a chef's knife to chop the spinach finely, then add it to the bowl. Add the egg and stir until fully incorporated. Cover and refrigerate until ready to use or for up to 2 days. Use the filling directly from the refrigerator. ›

---

1 package frozen or fresh filo dough sheets, each sheet about 12 by 17 inches (30 by 43 cm)

For the spinach–feta cheese filling

1 bunch spinach, about 1 lb (500 g)

1 tablespoon extra-virgin olive oil

1 cup thinly sliced green (spring) onions, white and tender green parts (page 40)

1 large clove garlic, minced (page 39)

3 tablespoons pine nuts, toasted (page 42), optional

¼ lb (125 g) feta cheese, patted dry

3 tablespoons raisins, optional

2 tablespoons minced fresh flat-leaf (Italian) parsley (page 42)

1 tablespoon minced fresh dill (page 42)

⅛ teaspoon freshly ground pepper

⅛ teaspoon freshly grated nutmeg (page 43)

1 large egg

4 tablespoons (2 oz/60 g) unsalted butter, or more if the filo dough is very dry

MAKES 24–36 PARCELS, OR 6–8 SERVINGS

CHEF'S TIP

I like to buy feta cheese at a deli where I can taste the different varieties and avoid any I feel are too salty. Greek and Bulgarian fetas are usually exceptional.

6 Assemble the tools and ingredients for the triangles

Filo dough dries out quickly when exposed to the air, so make sure you have all your ingredients and tools ready before removing the dough from the refrigerator. Line a large rimmed baking sheet (or 2 smaller ones) with parchment (baking) paper. Cover the baking sheet with a piece of plastic wrap. This sheet is for holding the finished filo triangles. Melt the butter in a small saucepan and let it cool slightly.

7 Ready the filo sheets

Tear off 2 sheets of plastic wrap, each about 2 feet (60 cm) long, and place them on the work surface, overlapping them side by side. Remove all the filo dough from the box and unroll it onto the plastic wrap. Cover the dough with 2 additional 2-foot-long sheets of plastic wrap, overlapping them in the center. Rinse 2 kitchen towels and wring them out. Place on top of the plastic wrap, covering the filo completely, but not touching it directly, or it will get soggy. (When finished, leave the plastic wrap on top of any remaining dough and roll up the dough. Wrap the dough in more plastic wrap, return it to the box, and refrigerate for up to 2 weeks.)

8 Butter a filo sheet

Although you will use only 6–9 sheets of filo dough, it is best to start with a whole package. If you are new to working with filo, it will seem very fragile and difficult to handle. You may need to discard some sheets, but the more you practice, the more comfortable you will become handling it. Carefully remove 1 filo sheet from the pile and place it on the work surface. Immediately re-cover the remaining filo sheets. Using a pastry brush, cover the entire filo sheet lightly with melted butter, dabbing it on and covering the edges well.

9 Cut the filo into strips

Using a ruler and a pastry wheel or sharp knife, cut the filo sheet lengthwise into 4 equal strips. Each strip will be about 3 inches (7.5 cm) wide. >

SHORTCUT

Use vacuum-packed filo dough, called yufka in Turkish, which is available in some Middle Eastern markets. This filo dough is precut into strips and ready to be folded into triangles.

10 Add the filling

Put about 1 tablespoon of the filling in the lower left-hand corner of 1 strip, placing it about ½ inch (12 mm) from both the bottom and the right edge. Don't be tempted to add more filling, which may cause the filling to leak out. Fold the bottom right corner of the filo strip over the filling so it reaches the left edge of the strip, forming a triangle. Using your fingers, gently pat the filling into the space.

MAKE-AHEAD TIP

To fill and fold filo triangles in advance, first line a tray with parchment (baking) paper. Place the triangles on the tray in a single layer, cover with plastic wrap, and refrigerate for up to 3 days. Or, place the tray in the freezer. When the triangles are frozen, transfer them to a heavy-duty locking plastic bag and freeze for up to 1 month. Bake the triangles directly from the refrigerator or freezer.

11 Fold up the triangle

Starting with the bottom left-hand corner, fold the triangle up along the left edge, retaining the triangular shape. Starting with the bottom left-hand corner, fold the triangle up to the right. Repeat in this fashion, folding carefully to maintain an even triangular shape, until you reach the top of the strip. To avoid seams on both sides of the triangle, I usually cut off the extra filo at the top, rather than fold it over onto the triangle. Place the finished triangle, seam side down, under the sheet of plastic wrap on the prepared baking sheet. Repeat the filling and folding steps with remaining strips, sheets of filo dough, and filling. Don't worry if there are some folded or crumbly parts. The filo parcels always bake up beautifully, hiding any folding flaws. Remelt the butter as necessary while working, adding additional butter if you run low.

12 Bake and serve the filo triangles

Preheat the oven to 400°F (200°C). Discard the plastic wrap from the baking sheet and rearrange the triangles, leaving space between them to allow room for them to puff up during baking. Brush the tops of the triangles generously with melted butter. Bake the triangles until brown and crisp, about 20 minutes. Transfer to a serving platter. Let stand for about 10 minutes before serving to allow the flavors to emerge.

Serving ideas

The shape of a filo packet is not limited to the triangle. After cutting a filo sheet into strips (see step 9), you can cut the strips into rectangles and wrap them around the filling to create beggar's purses or you can roll up the filling in the strips to form cylinders— two simple yet eye-catching ideas. Another way to vary the packets is to offer a second filling. The three-cheese mixture below is almost as popular as the classic spinach one.

Beggar's purses (top left)
Cut each filo strip into 3 equal rectangles. Position 1 rectangle horizontally. Stack 2 rectangles vertically on top, forming an X. Place 1¼ teaspoons filling in the center. Gather up the edges and twist to secure.

Cylinders (left)
Put 1½ teaspoons filling 1 inch (2.5 cm) from the short end of a filo strip. Roll the edge over the filling, fold over ¼ inch (6 mm) of both sides, and roll up.

Three-cheese filling (above)
In a food processor, pulse 4½ oz (140 g) *each* diced feta, Gruyère, and Brie cheese until mixed. Add a pinch *each* nutmeg and pepper, 1 large egg, and 1 tablespoon snipped fresh chives and mix well.

Onion & Cheese Turnovers

These turnovers call for enclosing a filling of gently cooked leeks, green onions, basil, and two types of cheese in a tender dough made with sour cream. Finishing the turnovers with a light brushing of beaten egg helps give the pretty half-moon pastries a shiny, golden brown finish.

1 Mix the dough

If you need help making turnover dough, turn to page 20. Fit a food processor with the metal blade and add the flours and salt. Pulse to combine the ingredients. Add the butter and process with on-off pulses until the butter has flattened into flakes and the rest of the mixture looks like grated Parmesan cheese, about 5 seconds. Using a rubber spatula, scrape down the sides of the work bowl. Add the sour cream and process with on-off pulses just until the mixture comes together in clumps; do not allow it to form a ball. (If you process the dough beyond this point, it will toughen.) Turn the dough out onto a lightly floured work surface. Using both hands and a bench scraper, gently push the dough together into a single mass and divide the dough in half. Shape each half into a flat rectangle about 3½ by 2½ inches (9 by 6 cm). Place the rectangles in separate locking plastic bags and refrigerate for at least 2 hours or up to 2 days.

2 Prepare the leek and green onions

If you are not sure how to prepare the leek or green onions, turn to page 40. First, rinse and slice the leek: Cut off the root end and the dark green top of the leek, leaving the white base and pale green top. Quarter the leek lengthwise and rinse well in a basin of water. Dry the leek with a kitchen towel, then thinly slice crosswise. Measure out ¾ cup (3½ oz/105 g) sliced leek. Then, slice the green onions: Trim off the root ends and tough green tops of the onions. Line up the onions and cut them crosswise into thin slices. Measure out ⅓ cup (1 oz/30 g) sliced green onions.

3 Cook the filling

Place a small, heavy frying pan over medium-low heat and add the olive oil. When the surface just shimmers, add the leek, cover, and cook, stirring occasionally, for about 5 minutes. Stir in the green onions, shallot, garlic, and basil, re-cover, and cook, stirring occasionally, until the leek, onions, shallot, and garlic are tender, about 5 minutes longer. Remove the leek mixture from the heat and let cool completely, about 30 minutes.

4 Finish the filling

Wash and dry the food processor, then add the mozzarella and Fontina cheeses and pulse until the cheeses are coarsely chopped. Add the salt, pepper, nutmeg, and 1 of the eggs and pulse just until the egg is fully incorporated. Stir the cheese mixture into the cooled leek mixture and mix in the chives. Set aside at room temperature. ▸

For the sour cream turnover dough

1 cup (5 oz/155 g) unbleached all-purpose (plain) flour

¼ cup (1 oz/30 g) cake (soft-wheat) flour

½ teaspoon kosher salt

½ cup (4 oz/125 g) cold unsalted butter, cut into 1-inch (2.5-cm) pieces

¼ cup (2 oz/60 g) cold sour cream

For the onion and cheese filling

1 small leek, about 6 oz (185 g)

3 green (spring) onions

1 tablespoon extra-virgin olive oil

1 small shallot, finely diced (page 38)

1 large clove garlic, minced (page 39)

½ cup (1½ oz/45 g) loosely packed coarsely chopped fresh basil (page 42)

3 oz (90 g) fresh whole-milk mozzarella cheese, drained, patted dry, and cut into 8 equal pieces

1½ oz (45 g) Fontina cheese, cut into 4 equal pieces

⅛ teaspoon kosher salt

Pinch of freshly ground pepper

Pinch of freshly grated nutmeg (page 43)

2 large eggs

2 teaspoons snipped fresh chives

1 teaspoon water for the egg wash

MAKES 28 TURNOVERS, OR 6–8 SERVINGS

5 Roll out the dough

If you are new to rolling out pastry dough, turn to page 31. Tear off 2 sheets of waxed paper, each about 15 inches (38 cm) long. Remove 1 dough rectangle from its bag, place it between the sheets on a work surface, and whack it several times with a heavy rolling pin to soften it. Roll out the dough lengthwise and crosswise, alternating directions and returning to the center each time, into a rectangle that measures 6 by 11 inches (15 by 28 cm). The dough should be about ⅛ inch (3 mm) thick. If the dough looks wrinkled, lift off the waxed paper and smooth it again over the dough. If the dough becomes too soft at any point, refrigerate it for about 15 minutes to firm it.

6 Cut out the pastry rounds

Remove the top piece of waxed paper and mark as many rounds as possible with a 3-inch (7.5-cm) pastry cutter (about 10). Re-cover the dough with the waxed paper, slip the dough and paper onto a baking sheet, and refrigerate while you roll and cut the second rectangle of dough in the same way.

7 Fill the pastry rounds

Have ready a cup of water. Line 1 large baking sheet (or 2 smaller ones) with parchment (baking) paper. Remove the first sheet of dough circles from the refrigerator and peel off the top sheet of waxed paper. Carefully peel the circles off the paper and place them next to one another on the paper-lined baking sheet. Return the paper with the pastry trimmings to the refrigerator. Spoon about 1½ teaspoons filling in the center of each pastry round. Using your finger, lightly moisten one-half of the edge of each round with water. Fold the coated edge of the round over the filling to meet the uncoated edge, making a half-moon. Press the ends together to seal tightly. Flatten the filling to distribute it evenly, if necessary. Repeat the filling process with the remaining rounds. Continue to fill the remaining dough circles on the second sheet. Then, reroll the trimmings, cut them into circles, fill, and place on the baking sheet(s). When all the turnovers are filled, seal the edges by pressing them together with the tines of a fork.

8 Chill the dough

Cover the turnovers with plastic wrap and refrigerate for at least 2 hours or up to 2 days. Chilling them discourages the cheese from leaking out during baking.

9 Bake and serve the turnovers

Preheat the oven to 400°F (200°C). In a small bowl, use a fork to mix the remaining egg and water; this is called an *egg wash*. Brush each turnover generously with some of the egg wash. Be careful it doesn't drip down the sides of the dough onto the pan; it can make the turnovers stick. Bake the turnovers until they are a rich golden brown, 20–25 minutes. Remove from the oven and, using a thin-lipped spatula, transfer them to a serving platter. Let the turnovers stand for about 10 minutes before serving, to allow the flavors to emerge.

Turnover Variations

Crisp, golden pockets of pastry dough can enclose almost any savory filling you like, and in many regions of the world, they do. Below are two distinctly different ethnic recipes, empanadas and samosas, that call for the same turnover techniques of rolling, filling, folding, and crimping the pastry rounds that you learned to make on pages 121–22. Many other filling possibilities exist, too, including a hearty mix of sausage and tomatoes. After trying the ideas here, you may want to devise your own combinations; just make sure the filling is thick enough, or it will leak out of its pastry wrapper in the heat of the oven. Each variation makes 28 turnovers, or 6 to 8 servings.

Empanadas

This popular Spanish recipe uses a spicy beef filling. Reserve any extra filling for another use.

Follow the recipe for Onion & Cheese Turnovers, replacing the filling with the one that follows.

To make the empanada filling: In a frying pan over medium-low heat, warm 1 tablespoon extra-virgin olive oil. Add 1 diced small yellow onion, cover, and sauté until translucent, about 10 minutes. Raise the heat to medium-high, add ½ lb (250 g) ground (minced) beef and cook, breaking up the meat, until no longer red, about 3 minutes. Add 1 minced jalapeño chile (or to taste), 1 minced large garlic clove, 1¼ teaspoons dried oregano, 1 teaspoon paprika, 1 teaspoon ground cumin, and 2 cups (16 fl oz/500 ml) tomato sauce. Bring to a boil and cook, stirring occasionally, until the sauce is almost completely absorbed and the mixture is thick, about 30 minutes.

Add ½ teaspoon kosher salt and ⅛ teaspoon freshly ground pepper. Adjust the seasonings. Let cool for 30 minutes, then mix in 1 large egg, 3 tablespoons raisins, 3 tablespoons chopped black or green olives, and 1 chopped hard-boiled egg (see page 91).

Samosas

Serve these Indian treats with chutney. Reserve any extra filling for another use.

Follow the recipe for Onion & Cheese Turnovers, replacing the filling with the one that follows.

To make the samosa filling: Place 2 peeled small russet potatoes in a saucepan and add salted water to cover. Bring to a boil, reduce the heat to medium, and simmer just until tender, 15–20 minutes. Drain, let cool, and finely dice.

In a nonstick frying pan over medium-low heat, warm 2 tablespoons olive oil. Add 1 diced small yellow onion and 1 minced jalapeño chile (or to taste), cover, and cook, stirring occasionally, for about 5 minutes. Add ½ teaspoon *each* freshly ground cumin seeds, coriander seeds, and fennel seeds; 1 tablespoon minced fresh ginger; and 2 minced large garlic cloves. Cover and sauté until the onion is soft, about 5 minutes. Add the diced potatoes and ¼ cup (¾ oz/20 g) frozen peas, cover, and cook, stirring occasionally and mashing gently, until very tender, about 6 minutes. Let cool. Add ½ teaspoon kosher salt, then adjust the seasonings. Stir in 1 tablespoon minced fresh cilantro (fresh coriander) and ¼ cup (2 oz/60 g) plain yogurt.

Sausage & Tomato Turnovers

These zesty sausage-and-tomato-filled half-moons are perfect for a cocktail party.

Follow the recipe for Onion & Cheese Turnovers, replacing the filling with the one that follows.

To make the sausage and tomato filling: In a frying pan over medium-low heat, sauté ⅔ cup (3½ oz/105 g) finely chopped andouille sausage until lightly browned, about 5 minutes. Using a slotted spoon, transfer the sausage to a bowl and reserve the drippings in the pan. Add 1 tablespoon olive oil, 1 diced yellow onion, and ½ cup (2½ oz/75 g) minced green bell pepper (capsicum) to the drippings and sauté over low heat until the onion is translucent, 6–8 minutes. Add 1 minced large garlic clove, ¼ teaspoon paprika, and ½ cup (4 fl oz/125 ml) tomato sauce and raise the heat to high. When the mixture comes to a boil, reduce the heat to medium and add the sausage. Let simmer, stirring occasionally, until the sauce is thick and most of the liquid has evaporated, about 20 minutes. Let the mixture cool, then transfer it to a food processor and process until finely chopped. Adjust the seasonings.

Bruschetta with Olives & Roasted Peppers

The Roman term *bruschetta* is used for relatively thick bread slices that have been grilled over a charcoal fire, then rubbed with the cut surface of a garlic clove and bathed in fragrant olive oil. The crisp slices are then served with a delicious topping such as the colorful, rustic mixture of bell pepper and olives used here.

1 Preheat the broiler or prepare a grill
If using the broiler (grill), place a rack as close to the heat source as possible and preheat the broiler. (Alternatively, for a more traditional approach, preheat a gas grill to high or prepare a medium-hot fire for direct grilling in a charcoal grill. Position the grill rack about 4 inches/10 cm above the fire.)

2 Roast the bell peppers
If you are not sure how to roast bell peppers, turn to page 44. If using the broiler, line a rimmed baking sheet with aluminum foil. Arrange the bell peppers on the lined baking sheet and broil (grill), turning until blistered and blackened on all sides, about 15 minutes. (If using the grill, arrange the peppers on the grill rack and roast, turning as needed, until the skin is blistered and blackened on all sides, 8–10 minutes.) Transfer the peppers to a paper bag and close loosely. This allows the peppers to steam as they cool, which loosens the skin from the flesh, making them easier to peel.

3 Peel, seed, and chop the peppers
Remove the peppers from the bag. Using your fingers, peel off the skin from each pepper. Do not be concerned if a little skin clings to the flesh. It is tempting to run the pepper under water to hasten this process, but the pepper is more flavorful if it isn't diluted by rinsing. Lay the peppers on a cutting board, preferably one with a groove around its perimeter (peppers have a lot of juices), and slit each pepper lengthwise. Open each pepper flat and cut around the stem and remove it. Then, remove the seeds and ribs. Use paper towels to help soak up excess juices or to wipe out any clinging seeds. Pat the peppers dry. Using a chef's knife, coarsely chop the peppers. Transfer to a medium ceramic or glass bowl.

4 Pit and chop the olives
If you need help pitting the olives, turn to page 35. Place the olives in a locking plastic bag, force out the air, seal closed, and gently pound with a meat pounder or a rolling pin to loosen the pits. Remove the crushed olives from the bag and separate the pits from the olive flesh with your fingers. For stubborn olives, use a paring knife to cut the flesh from the pits. Using the chef's knife, finely chop the olives. You should have about ⅓ cup finely chopped olives. Set aside. ›

For the olive and pepper topping

3 large red or orange bell peppers (capsicums), about 7 oz (220 g) each

⅔ cup (3 oz/90 g) Kalamata olives

1 small orange

2 or 3 sprigs fresh basil

2 or 3 sprigs fresh mint

2 tablespoons extra-virgin olive oil

¼ teaspoon kosher salt

For the bruschetta

16–24 slices baguette, cut on the diagonal ½ inch (12 mm) thick

6 large cloves garlic, halved lengthwise

About ¼ cup (2 fl oz/60 ml) extra-virgin olive oil

1 green (spring) onion

MAKES 4–6 SERVINGS

5 Zest and juice the orange

To find out more about how to zest and juice citrus, turn to page 43. First, zest the orange: Using a fine rasp grater, remove the colored part of the peel from the orange, taking care not to grate the bitter white pith underneath. Then, juice the orange: Cut the orange in half crosswise and, using a handheld reamer or a citrus juicer, squeeze out the juice and measure 2 tablespoons.

6 Mince the herbs

If you need help mincing herbs, turn to page 42. Remove the leaves from the basil sprigs and discard the stems. Gather the leaves into a small pile. Holding down the knife tip with one hand, chop the basil, moving the blade up and down in a rhythmic motion until the leaves are uniformly chopped into very fine pieces, or *minced*. Measure out 1 teaspoon minced basil. Repeat to mince the mint and measure out 1 teaspoon.

7 Mix the topping

Add the orange zest and juice to the bowl with the peppers and mix well with a fork. Stir in the olive oil, olives, basil, mint, and salt, mixing well. Taste and adjust the seasonings with salt. Cover the bowl and let the topping stand for at least 30 minutes at room temperature or up to overnight in the refrigerator to blend the flavors. If refrigerated, bring to room temperature before serving.

8 Broil or grill the bread slices

If broiling, preheat the broiler. Arrange the bread slices on a large baking sheet, slide under the broiler, and broil, turning once, until lightly browned on both sides, 3–4 minutes total. (If grilling, preheat the gas grill to medium-high or add hot charcoal to the grill to bring the fire up to medium-hot, if necessary. Arrange the bread slices on the grill rack and grill, turning once and watching closely to avoid burning, until lightly browned on both sides, 2–3 minutes total.) The interior of the slices should still be soft. Arrange the broiled or grilled bread slices on a large rimmed baking sheet in a single layer.

9 Flavor the bread slices

When cool enough to handle, rub both sides of each bread slice with the cut side of a garlic clove half. Drizzle the olive oil evenly over the bread slices. Let the bread stand for several minutes to absorb the oil.

10 Finish the topping and adjust the seasonings

For more details on slicing the green onion, turn to page 40. Trim off the root end and tough green top of the onion. Thinly slice the onion crosswise. Stir three-fourths of the onion into the topping. Taste the topping; if you feel it tastes dull, stir in a bit more salt until you are happy with the flavor balance.

11 Assemble and serve the bruschetta

Spread 1–2 tablespoons of the topping onto each toast. Arrange on a serving platter, garnish with the remaining green onion, and serve right away.

Bruschetta Variations

In Italy, bruschetta is a popular hors d'oeuvre, or antipasto, and after you have made the recipe on page 125, you will understand why. The crisp toasts, fragrant with garlic and olive oil, are simple to make and provide a delicious base that complements many toppings. Combine the unique flavors of figs, prosciutto, and Gorgonzola any time. Or, assemble a classic Mediterranean pairing of roasted tomatoes and goat cheese whenever fresh tomatoes are available, or a mixture of asparagus and ricotta in spring when the green spears are in season. After trying the toppings below, you will be ready to experiment with some combinations of your own. Each variation makes 4 to 6 servings.

Fig, Prosciutto & Gorgonzola Bruschetta

Marinating the figs in balsamic vinegar softens them and deepens their flavor.

In a small bowl, combine 10 stemmed and thinly sliced dried Black Mission figs, about 2½ oz (75 g) total weight, and 2 tablespoons balsamic vinegar. Let stand at room temperature, stirring occasionally, for at least 2 hours or up to overnight.

Next, in a small bowl, use a fork to mash together 3 oz (90 g) room-temperature Gorgonzola or other blue cheese and 3 oz (90 g) room-temperature cream cheese until smooth. Stir in 1 tablespoon snipped fresh chives. Cut 3 thin slices prosciutto (1 oz/30 g) into thin slivers and set aside.

Prepare the bread slices as directed in steps 8 and 9. Spread the cheese mixture onto the toasts. Top each toast with 3 or 4 fig slices and several slivers of prosciutto. Serve right away.

Tomato & Goat Cheese Bruschetta

Layer goat cheese and thyme with roasted tomatoes for a Provençal bruschetta.

Preheat the oven to 325°F (165°C). Line a rimmed baking sheet with aluminum foil. Cut 6 plum (Roma) tomatoes lengthwise into quarters. Remove the seeds and cores. Place the tomatoes in a bowl and toss with 2 tablespoons extra-virgin olive oil, ⅛ teaspoon kosher salt, and ⅛ teaspoon freshly ground pepper. Arrange the tomatoes, skin side down, on the baking sheet and roast until reduced in size but still moist, about 1½ hours. In a small frying pan over low heat, warm 1 tablespoon olive oil. Add 2 tablespoons minced shallot and 1 minced large garlic clove and sauté until softened, 3–4 minutes. Let cool.

Next, in a small bowl, use a fork to mash ¼ lb (125 g) room-temperature fresh goat cheese. Mix in 1–2 tablespoons whole milk, adding just enough so the cheese is spreadable. Stir in the shallot mixture and 1 teaspoon minced fresh thyme. Season with kosher salt and pepper.

Prepare the bread slices as directed in steps 8 and 9. Spread the cheese mixture onto the toasts, then top with the tomatoes, skin side up. Serve right away.

Asparagus & Ricotta Bruschetta

Lemon zest and juice heighten the flavors in this simple topping.

Snap off the tough ends of 9 asparagus spears. Toss the spears with 1 teaspoon extra-virgin olive oil.

Preheat a broiler (grill) or ready a grill. Place the spears on a rimmed baking sheet or the grill grate and cook, turning once, until tender, about 3 minutes. Let cool, then cut into ¼-inch (6-mm) slices.

Next, in a bowl, combine ¾ cup (6 oz/185 g) room-temperature whole-milk ricotta cheese, 2 teaspoons grated lemon zest, and 2 teaspoons fresh lemon juice. Stir in ¼ cup (2 fl oz/60 ml) extra-virgin olive oil, 1 tablespoon minced fresh basil, 1 tablespoon minced fresh tarragon, ½ teaspoon kosher salt, ⅛ teaspoon freshly ground pepper, and the asparagus. Adjust the seasonings.

Prepare the bread slices as directed in steps 8 and 9. Thinly slice 1 green (spring) onion (white and tender green parts). Stir three-fourths of the green onion into the asparagus mixture. Spread the cheese mixture onto the toasts, then sprinkle with the remaining green onion. Serve right away.

Broiled Stuffed Clams

Here, clams are steamed in a fragrant mixture of white wine, garlic, shallot, and butter that lightly infuses them with flavor. The same potent mixture is used to bind the chopped clam meat with aromatic basil and bread crumbs for the stuffing, which cooks to a crisp and golden brown finish in a hot broiler.

24 hard-shelled clams in the shell, 1¾–2 lb (750 g–1 kg) total weight

1 tablespoon kosher salt

1 cup (8 fl oz/250 ml) dry white wine such as Sauvignon Blanc or Chardonnay

1 tablespoon unsalted butter, cut into small pieces

1 tablespoon extra-virgin olive oil

3 large cloves garlic, quartered lengthwise

1 shallot, thinly sliced

1 small bay leaf

⅛ teaspoon red pepper flakes, optional

½ cup (2 oz/60 g) fine dried bread crumbs (page 47)

1 green (spring) onion, white and tender green parts, halved lengthwise and thinly sliced crosswise

1½ tablespoons minced fresh basil (page 42)

About 2 tablespoons freshly grated Parmigiano-Reggiano cheese

MAKES 4–6 SERVINGS

MAKE-AHEAD TIP
The clams can be steamed, stuffed, and sprinkled with the cheese up to 2 hours in advance. Set them aside at room temperature until ready to cook. They may also be prepared up to 1 day in advance. Keep them covered and refrigerated, then cook them directly from the refrigerator.

1 **Soak the clams**
Scrub the clam shells with a stiff brush under running cool water. Fill a large bowl with water to a depth of 4 inches (10 cm). Add the salt and stir until dissolved. Add the clams and let soak for 30 minutes. If the water is sandy, drain the clams and soak a second time. Drain the clams and discard any open clams that do not close to the touch. Rinse the bowl and place near the stove.

2 **Steam the clams**
Pour the wine into a nonreactive frying pan large enough to hold the clams in a single layer. Add the butter, olive oil, garlic, shallot, bay leaf, and the pepper flakes, if using, and place over medium-high heat. Stir until the butter melts. Add the clams and reduce the heat so the liquid gently bubbles, or simmers. Cover and cook, shaking the pan occasionally, for 3 minutes. Uncover and, using tongs, transfer any clams that have opened to the bowl, shaking the shells to drain their liquid back into the pan. Continue cooking, uncovered, until the remaining clams open, about 2 minutes; remove them as they open. If any unopened clams remain, re-cover the pan and cook for 2–3 minutes longer. Discard any clams that fail to open. Strain the cooking liquid through a fine-mesh sieve set over a small bowl.

3 **Shell the clams and make the stuffing**
Carefully break off one the shells of each clam, rinse the empty shells, and arrange, hollow side up, in a large baking dish in a single layer. Using a paring knife, free the clams from the remaining shells. Discard these remaining shells after removing the clams. Dice the clam meat into ½-inch (12-mm) pieces. Place in a bowl and add the bread crumbs, green onion, and basil. Slowly stir in the strained clam liquid, adding just enough (4–5 tablespoons/2–3 fl oz/60–80 ml) for the mixture to stick together. Taste and adjust the seasonings; add a little salt or more red pepper flakes or basil until you are happy with the flavor balance.

4 **Stuff the clams**
Spoon about 1 teaspoon of the clam mixture into each of the shells in the baking dish. Sprinkle with a generous pinch of the grated cheese and spoon any remaining liquid over the tops.

5 **Broil and serve the clams**
Position the rack as close to the heat source as possible and preheat the broiler (grill). Broil (grill) the clams until the filling is brown and crisp, 3–5 minutes. Serve right away directly from the baking dish. Provide guests with small plates, demitasse or other small spoons, and a bowl for discarding the empty shells.

Gougères

The use of milk in the dough for these savory cream puffs, laced with buttery, nutty Gruyère cheese, enriches and softens the finished pastry. The puffs expand dramatically in the heat of the oven, creating crisp, golden brown bitefuls that taste best when eaten hot.

1 Make the dough

In a small, heavy stainless-steel saucepan over medium heat, stir together the milk, salt, nutmeg, and butter. Bring to a boil, stirring occasionally. As soon as you see steady, rigorous bubbles forming in the liquid, remove it from the heat and add the flour all at once. Using a heatproof silicone spatula, stir vigorously until the mixture is smooth, pulls away from the sides of the pan, and forms a rough ball, 15–20 seconds. Return to medium heat and continue stirring just until a film of flour begins to form on the pan bottom, about 20 seconds. Transfer the dough to the bowl of a stand mixer fitted with the paddle attachment. Beat the dough until it is just warm to the touch, 3–4 minutes.

2 Mix in the eggs and cheese

Add 1 egg and beat on low speed until fully incorporated. Add 2 more eggs, one at a time, in the same way. Lift the dough with the spatula; it should look wet and hold soft peaks that droop gently. If not, beat the fourth egg in a small bowl and add to the dough 1 tablespoon at a time, repeating the test after each addition. You will probably need only half of this egg. Stir in the diced and grated cheeses.

3 Shape the puffs

Position racks in the upper third and lower middle of the oven and preheat to 400°F (200°C). Grease 2 large rimmed baking sheets with butter. If you are new to using a pastry (piping) bag, turn to page 30. Fit a pastry bag with a ½-inch (12-mm) plain round tip, and fill the bag with the dough. Holding the bag straight up over a prepared pan, squeeze out a mound 1 inch (2.5 cm) tall and 1¼ inches (3 cm) in diameter. Stop squeezing, twirl the bag to break off the tip of dough, and pipe the next mound in the same way, spacing them about 1½ inches (4 cm) apart. Using a fingertip, gently flatten any tips. Whisk the egg with the water to make an *egg wash*. Brush each puff with the egg wash. Be careful it doesn't drip down the sides of the puffs onto the pan; it can keep the puffs from rising.

4 Bake and serve the puffs

Bake the puffs until they are almost doubled in size and firm to the touch, 25–30 minutes. After 15 minutes, switch the baking sheets between the racks and rotate them 180 degrees so they bake evenly. Reduce the oven temperature to 375°F (190°C) and continue to bake until golden brown, 10–12 minutes longer. Remove the sheets with the puffs and turn off the oven. Sprinkle the puffs with the Parmigiano-Reggiano cheese, then using the tip of a small, sharp knife, make a small slit in the side of each puff. Return the sheets with the puffs to the oven and leave the oven door open. Let the puffs dry in the oven for 10–12 minutes, then transfer them to a platter or serving basket. Serve right away.

For the dough

1 cup (8 fl oz/250 ml) whole milk

½ teaspoon kosher salt

⅛ teaspoon freshly grated nutmeg (page 43)

6 tablespoons (3 oz/90 g) cold unsalted butter, cut into 12 equal pieces

1 cup (5 oz/150 g) unbleached all-purpose (plain) flour

3–4 large eggs, at room temperature

¼ lb (125 g) Gruyère cheese, finely diced

2 tablespoons freshly grated Parmigiano-Reggiano cheese

Unsalted butter, at room temperature, for preparing the baking sheets

1 large egg or leftover beaten egg from dough

1 teaspoon water

2 tablespoons freshly grated Parmigiano-Reggiano cheese

MAKES FORTY-FIVE 2-INCH (5-CM) ROUND PASTRIES, OR 8–10 SERVINGS

CHEF'S TIP

It's often easier to incorporate eggs using a mixer than by hand with a spatula. Just be sure to run the mixer on low speed so you don't beat in too much air. You don't want to use a food processor for the same reason. A stand mixer fitted with a flat paddle attachment also works better than a handheld mixer, which has beaters where the dough can lodge.

Using Key Tools & Equipment

Equipping your kitchen with the basics—sharp knives, a well-chosen collection of cookware, and such all-purpose kitchen tools as sturdy measuring cups and a reliable vegetable peeler—will give you a good start toward successful cooking. When making hors d'oeuvres, a food processor will also make many recipes easier. Below you'll find tips for using these and other tools to help you produce the best results every time you cook.

Food Processors, Blenders & Mixers

A food processor is versatile, good for both puréeing ingredients as well as mixing doughs. It comes with various disks and blades for other tasks, such as slicing and chopping vegetables and grating cheese. A blender is excellent for puréeing, too, delivering a creamier texture than a food processor. A stand mixer fitted with the paddle attachment is ideal for making the dough for Gougères (page 131). You can also whip egg whites with its whip attachment, or you can use a handheld electric mixer.

Grating, Grinding & Juicing Tools

Freshly grated cheese and citrus zest and freshly ground spices will always yield the best flavor. A multisided box grater-shredder gives you a choice of very fine to coarse rasps. Long, flat rasp graters are available in several sizes for zesting citrus and grating fresh ginger, hard cheeses, or nutmeg. A handheld reamer comes in handy for extracting a few drops or more of citrus juice. Since almost every savory dish requires freshly ground pepper, a sturdy pepper mill is a must for every kitchen. You will also taste the difference when you grind whole fresh spices in a spice grinder or an electric coffee grinder. Reserve this coffee grinder just for spices and brush it out between uses. (A mortar with a pestle is an good alternative.)

Measuring Tools

It's important always to measure your ingredients to ensure the correct volume, proportions, and seasonings. Use metal cups with level tops for dry ingredients; first fill them and then level off the top with the back of a knife. Use clear glass or plastic measuring cups with spouts for

liquids and read them at eye level. Measuring spoons ranging from ¼ teaspoon to 1 tablespoon are perfect for measuring small amounts of either wet or dry ingredients. A ruler is useful when working with filo or pastry dough.

Colanders, Sieves & Spinners

Use a metal colander for rinsing and draining blanched vegetables, salting eggplant, or draining cooked spinach. A sieve coupled with cheesecloth (muslin) helps strain every last bit of grit from clam juice and mushroom liquid. A lettuce spinner efficiently dries rinsed greens and herbs and quickly removes excess water from potato slices for chips.

Knives & Slicers

Good, sharp knives are critical to kitchen success. It's frustrating and difficult to cut food with a dull or improperly sized knife. You need an 8-inch (20-cm) chef's knife (the measure is the blade length) for general cutting and chopping, and a 3½- to 4-inch (9- to 10-cm) paring knife for trimming and mincing. A serrated knife easily slices breads, and a long carving knife comes in handy for slicing fish such as Gravlax (page 87).

To reduce the time needed to slice vegetables and other foods thinly such as potatoes for chips, invest in a mandoline or mandoline-style kitchen slicer.

Pastry Tools

When making pastry, it's best to use a cold work surface such as marble. It should be low enough for you to exert pressure easily while rolling out dough with a heavy rolling pin. A metal bench scraper efficiently cuts pastry dough and cleans surfaces. Pastry cutters come in sets, and a 3-inch (7.5-cm) round size is perfect for the turnovers in this book. A pastry wheel or pizza cutter easily cuts filo dough. You'll also need a pastry brush for brushing on melted butter.

Mixing Bowls

Graduated sets of tempered glass or metal mixing bowls will include all the sizes you need, and they are easy to store. Use the smallest bowls to measure out the seasonings for your *mise en place*.

Baking Pans and Molds

Rimmed baking sheets are useful for toasting bread and baking tartlets. Have small barquette or tartlet molds for making tartlets or use miniature muffin pans. You can rely on more common tools as well. A wire rack set on a rimmed baking sheet becomes a broiler pan for skewers. A deep roasting pan can hold the water needed to gently bake a pâté.

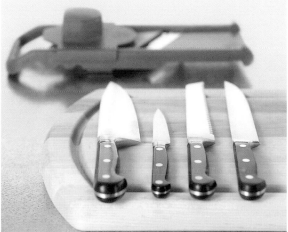

Saucepans & Frying Pans

Heavy, well-made saucepans with stainless-steel or other nonreactive interiors are best because they distribute heat evenly and can be used to cook acidic foods such as tomatoes. Copper and aluminum are both good heat conductors, and one of them is often sandwiched between layers of stainless steel in high-quality cookware. Buy a 6- to 8-quart (6- to 8-l) deep, heavy multi-purpose pot with a lid for cooking beans or spinach. Other useful pans include 2-quart (2-l) and 4-quart (4-l) heavy saucepans with lids. Use them to hard-boil eggs or in combination with a collapsible steamer basket to cook or blanch vegetables. A smaller saucepan is perfect for melting butter.

Heavy 10- and 12-inch (25- and 30-cm) frying pans are used for toasting nuts, sautéing onions and shallots, and many other uses. Look for ovenproof handles, and have at least one pan with a nonstick surface (which is easy to clean). Use a cast-iron frying pan or griddle, if you have one, when cooking blini; the heavy iron retains heat and cooks at an even temperature.

Tools for Prepping Ingredients

As with much of cooking, when making hors d'oeuvres, a good deal of your time will be spent preparing ingredients. A mushroom brush and a small, stiff brush for scrubbing clams or potatoes are useful, and you will need a sharp, sturdy vegetable peeler with a comfortable handle for making crudités such as raw carrot sticks and cucumber slices.

A melon baller makes quick work of scooping out a bit of flesh from small cooked potatoes. Similarly, a tomato corer can be used to scoop out the seed sacs from cherry tomatoes. Use a bar-style lemon stripper to strip away thin strips of green skin for decorative fluted cucumber slices. Oyster knives have thick handles for easy gripping, and their sturdy, dull blades are ideal for slipping between oyster shells and levering them open.

Frying Equipment

When deep-frying—particularly tortilla or potato chips—you can use a wok or heavy, deep saucepan for heating the oil. A deep-frying thermometer is a must for maintaining the correct oil temperature; oil that is too hot may flare up; while oil that is too cool will yield soggy results. Use a metal or mesh skimmer for turning foods in the oil and for removing them when they are finished frying.

Spoons, Whisks & Spatulas

It's good to have a wide assortment of spoons, whisks, and spatulas in your kitchen. You'll need a regular wire whisk for blini batter, vinaigrettes, or smoothing out dips and a balloon whisk for beating egg whites. Use a slotted spoon to transfer cooked beans or fried bacon bits when you want to leave the cooking liquid or excess fat behind. Wooden spoons are good for general stirring and blending; have at least one with a flat bottom to get into the corners of pans. A heatproof silicone spatula is useful for folding ingredients, filling pastry bags, and general mixing—and since it can withstand high temperatures up to 500°F (260°C), you can even use it to stir hot mixtures on the stove. Use a small ladle to portion out the batter for blini, and a thin-lipped, metal spatula to flip them.

Piping Tools

You may not immediately associate piping tools with hors d'oeuvres, but if you make hors d'oeuvres often, a pastry bag and set of tips will give many of your presentations a professional look.

Baking Dishes

Baking dishes, often made from ovenproof porcelain or earthenware, are usually pretty enough to go from oven to table. This book calls for a flameproof gratin dish and 4-cup (32–fl oz/1-l) terrine.

Serving Dishes & Tools

Have plenty of flat baskets, platters, and bowls on hand for serving. Provide small spreaders for guests if serving tapenade or pâté. Small plates and cocktail forks or demitasse spoons should accompany items that may be difficult to pick up.

Kitchen Linens

Pot holders are a must for handling hot pans and dishes. Select washable ones that easily conform to your hand. Sturdy kitchen towels can also protect your hands when removing hot dishes or shucking oysters, and are indispensible for kitchen cleanup. You can also use them to cover food while it is resting and to keep filo dough from drying out.

Miscellaneous Equipment

A meat pounder will help you flatten chicken breasts and also help you pound olives when you need to remove the pits. Spring-loaded tongs are a cook's second pair of hands. You will come to use them every day for sautéing and frying. Use kitchen scissors to snip chives quickly. A pair of small tweezers is useful for pulling out fish bones.

Glossary

ANCHOVIES These tiny, silver-skinned fish appear widely in Mediterranean cooking and are a traditional ingredient in Tapenade (page 63). Anchovy fillets packed in olive oil are commonly available in tins, but look for higher-quality fillets sold in glass jars.

ARUGULA Also known as rocket, these slender, green, deeply notched leaves have a nutty, slightly peppery taste. Larger leaves will be more pungent than smaller ones.

AVOCADOS Rich in flavor and texture, two major varieties of avocado are commonly available: California's dark green, dimpled Hass avocado and the smoother, paler green Fuerte. Hass avocados boast the highest oil content and will produce the best results in Guacamole (page 60).

BEANS, DRIED
Known collectively as legumes along with peas and lentils, dried beans are among the world's most healthful foods.

Black These small beans are uniformly black with a shiny surface. They are used widely in Latin American cooking.

Cannellini Ivory in color, these dried beans have a smooth texture and are a traditional ingredient in Italian cooking.

Chickpea Rich and nutty tasting, these large beige beans, also known as garbanzo or ceci beans, have a firm texture.

Fava Also called broad beans, English beans, or horse beans, these large, light brown beans have a slightly bitter taste and grainy texture. Look for dried split yellow fava beans at Middle Eastern markets.

Pinto These pale brown beans have darker, sometimes pinkish streaks that disappear when cooked and a full, earthy flavor.

White This term refers to a group of beans that includes Great Northern beans, navy beans, kidney beans, and cannellini. They are mild with a creamy texture.

BELGIAN ENDIVE These pale, tightly furled, slightly conical shoots are also known as witloof or chicory. They are grown by a labor-intensive method that requires the roots to sprout in a cool, dark space in order to keep the green chlorophyll from developing. Although most endives are creamy white with just a touch of yellowish green at the edges, a variety with pale burgundy tips is also available.

BREAD CRUMBS Use plain fine dried bread crumbs to lend body to stuffings such as the one used to make Broiled Stuffed Clams (page 128). You can easily make dried bread crumbs at home (page 47) or purchase them, often sold in canisters, at the supermarket. If you buy them, do not pick seasoned crumbs, which contain salt, dried herbs, and cheese.

BUTTER, UNSALTED Butter that is unsalted is preferable to salted because it allows you more control over the seasoning of a dish. When making pastry dough, seek out European-style unsalted butter, which has a higher butterfat content and will coat the flour more easily. Refrigerate unsalted butter in its original wrapping for up to 6 weeks.

CAPERS The unopened flower buds of bushes native to the Mediterranean, capers are dried, cured, and then usually packed in a vinegar brine. Rinse them briefly and blot dry before using.

CAVIAR The roe (eggs) of various members of the sturgeon family, caviar is one of the world's most prized culinary luxuries. In the past, the best caviar has come from three types of sturgeon that swim in the Caspian Sea: beluga, osetra, and sevruga. In recent years, these sturgeon have become increasingly endangered, and caviar exports from this region are becoming more limited. Fortunately, top-quality caviar from farmed sturgeon in areas such as California, Iran, and Romania is available. Although they aren't "true" caviar, other delicious fish roe are available, among them the eggs of salmon, whitefish, and trout.

CAYENNE A very hot ground red pepper made from dried cayenne and other chiles, cayenne is used sparingly to add heat or to heighten flavor. Always begin with a very small amount and add more to taste in small increments.

CHEESES
Cheeses for hors d'oeuvres include smooth varieties you can pipe, others that melt well in fillings, and those packed with flavor.

Feta A young cheese traditionally made from sheep's milk and known for its crumbly texture. Feta's saltiness is heightened by the brine in which the cheese is packed.

Fontina This Italian cow's milk cheese has a mild taste, slightly creamy texture, and a light but heady aroma.

Goat Made from pure goat's milk, or a blend of goat's and cow's milk, fresh goat cheese is creamy and tangy. Montrachet, a well-known variety, is soft and spreadable.

Gorgonzola A cow's milk blue cheese with a creamy texture and a pleasantly pungent flavor. When young, it is creamy, soft, and mildly pungent. This version is usually labeled Gorgonzola *dolcelatte* or *dolce*.

Gruyère This semifirm, dense, smooth cow's milk cheese is produced in Switzerland and France and is appreciated for its mild, nutty flavor and superior melting properties.

Mozzarella This mild, creamy cheese made from cow's milk or water buffalo's milk is formed into balls. Seek out fresh mozzarella, which is sold surrounded by some of its whey, rather than the dry vacuum-sealed cheeses.

Parmigiano-Reggiano The "true" Parmesan cheese, this is an aged, hard grating cheese made from partially skimmed cow's milk. It has a salty flavor and a rich, assertive fragrance. It is produced in the Italian region of Emilia-Romagna. Its rind is labeled with its trademarked name, Parmigiano-Reggiano.

Pecorino Romano A pleasantly salty Italian sheep's milk cheese with a grainy texture, *pecorino romano* is sharp and pungent.

Ricotta This soft, mild cheese sold in plastic tubs is made by heating the whey left over from making pecorino and other cheeses.

Roquefort France's premier blue cheese, Roquefort is made from sheep's milk. Pale, moist, and crumbly, Roquefort has a strong, salty, peppery flavor.

CHILE POWDER A pure powder made by grinding a single specific variety of dried chile. Ancho and New Mexico chile powders are the most common. Seek out chipotle chile powder for a particularly smoky flavor. Do not confuse chile powder with chili powder, typically a blend of powdered dried chile, oregano, cumin, and other seasonings.

CLAMS, HARD-SHELLED Clams are either hard shelled or soft shelled, and different varieties are found in the Atlantic and the Pacific. Atlantic hard-shelled clams are called quahogs and come in various sizes, from small littlenecks to large chowder clams. On the Pacific coast, you'll find unrelated hard-shelled littlenecks. Buy the freshest clams you can from a reputable fish merchant. The clams should not be open—if one gaps a little, prod it gently. If it does not close immediately, do not buy it.

CREAM, HEAVY A key ingredient in the custard fillings for savory tartlets (page 107), heavy cream is also known as double cream and is often labeled "heavy whipping cream." It is high in milk fat, which gives the cream its ultrarich taste.

CREAM OF TARTAR This white powder is potassium tartrate, a by-product of wine making. It was once a common leavening agent for breads made without yeast, but today is more often used to stabilize egg whites when beating.

CRÈME FRAÎCHE A soured cultured cream product, originally from France, crème fraîche is similar to sour cream. Silken and thick, it is tangy and sweet, with a hint of nuttiness

CURRY POWDER Typical ingredients in this ground spice blend from South Asia include turmeric, cumin, coriander, pepper, cardamom, mustard, cloves, and ginger. Curry powders are categorized as mild, hot, and very hot. Madras curry powder is a well-balanced version with medium heat.

EDAMAME The Japanese term for soybeans harvested while still young, plump, and green. *Edamame* are sold frozen or fresh and already shelled in many supermarkets. You can buy them fresh at farmers' markets, too.

FENNEL This Mediterranean vegetable has a sweet, faintly aniselike flavor and is similar to celery in appearance and texture. Choose rounded fennel bulbs, rather than the flatter oval elongated bulbs, which may be more fibrous. To prepare it, cut the stalks off the bulb, then using a paring knife, remove the fibrous, blemished outer layer of the bulb. Halve the bulb lengthwise and cut out the thick central core and discard it.

FIG, BLACK MISSION Small and sweet, Black Mission figs are one of more than 150 fig varieties. When ripe, they have a deep purple-black color and should feel soft, but not squishy, when gently pressed.

FLOUR
When we think of flour, we most often think of all-purpose (plain) flour ground from wheat. However, there are many different types of flour, and they may be milled from a variety of grains and other foods.

All-purpose Two general types of wheat are grown: hard wheat, which is higher in gluten, and soft wheat, which has less gluten and more starch. All-purpose, or plain, flour is a mixture of the two flours. Unbleached flour has a better flavor and silkier texture than bleached flour.

Buckwheat Made by milling the seeds of an herb, this dark flour has a nutty, slightly sweet taste and firm texture.

Cake Milled from soft wheat and containing cornstarch (cornflour), cake flour is high in starch and low in gluten, the elastic protein that makes dough difficult to roll.

GINGER A refreshing combination of spicy and sweet in both aroma and flavor, ginger adds a lively note to many recipes, particularly Asian dishes. Select ginger that is firm and heavy and has smooth skin.

HERBS
Using fresh herbs is one of the best things you can do to improve your cooking. Dried herbs do have their place, but fresh herbs usually bring brighter flavors to a dish.

Basil Used in kitchens throughout the Mediterranean and in Southeast Asia, fresh basil adds a highly aromatic, peppery flavor.

Bay These elongated gray-green leaves are often used to season cooking liquids, imparting a slightly sweet, citrusy, nutty flavor. Usually sold dried, bay leaves should be removed from a dish before serving.

Chives These slender, hollow, grasslike blades are used to give an onionlike flavor to dishes, without the bite.

Cilantro Also called fresh coriander or Chinese parsley, cilantro has a bright astringent taste. It is used extensively in Mexican, Asian, Indian, Latin, and Middle Eastern cuisines.

Dill This herb has fine, feathery leaves with a distinct aromatic taste. Dill is often used in savory pastries and fillings.

Marjoram This Mediterranean herb has a milder flavor than its cousin, oregano. It is best used fresh.

Mint This refreshing herb is available in many varieties, with spearmint the most commonly found.

Oregano This aromatic, spicy herb is also known as wild marjoram. It is one of the few herbs that keeps its flavor well when dried.

Parsley, flat-leaf This dark green Italian variety of the faintly peppery herb adds vibrant color and pleasing flavor to many hors d'oeuvres.

Rosemary This woody Mediterranean herb, with leaves like pine needles, has an assertive flavor. Always use in moderation.

Sage These soft, gray-green leaves are sweet and aromatic. Sage is a common addition to northern Italian dishes.

Tarragon With its slender, deep green leaves and elegant, aniselike scent, tender tarragon is commonly used in French cooking.

JALAPEÑO CHILE This fresh hot chile measures 2–4 inches (5–10 cm) long, has a generous amount of flesh, and ranges from mildly hot to fiery.

LEEKS A sweet and mild-flavored member of the onion family, a leek is long and cylindrical with a pale white root end and dark green leaves. The green leaves are tough; most recipes use only the white and sometimes the pale green parts. Be sure to rinse leeks well to remove any grit lodged between the layers of their leaves.

MUSHROOMS
Before using mushrooms, clean off any dirt with a damp cloth or soft brush. Trim away the dried end of the tender stems, or if the stem is tough, remove it completely.

Cremini Also known as Italian or Roman mushrooms or common brown mushrooms, these small cultivated mushrooms mature to become portobellos.

Porcini Fresh porcini, also called ceps, have a sweet fragrance and full, earthy taste. They are rarely found fresh, so many recipes call for the dried version—a good substitute.

Shiitake These popular Japanese mushrooms are now widely cultivated. Be sure to remove the thin, tough stems before using.

White This variety is the cultivated all-purpose mushroom stocked in most markets. It is sometimes called a button mushroom.

MUSTARD, DIJON Originating in Dijon, France, this silky smooth and slightly tangy mustard contains brown or black mustard seeds, white wine, and herbs.

NONREACTIVE A term used to describe a pan or dish made of or lined with a material—stainless steel, enamel, ceramic, and glass—that will not react with acidic ingredients, such as citrus juice or tomatoes.

NUTMEG The seed of a tropical evergreen tree, a nutmeg has a hard shell and is about ¾ inch (2 cm) long. Buy the slightly sweet spice whole and grate it just before using.

OIL
The heat requirements and other ingredients of a recipe usually suggest which oil is appropriate to use. As a general rule, choose less refined, more flavorful oils for uncooked uses such as drizzling, tossing, and dressing, and refined, blander oils for cooking.

Asian sesame This amber-colored oil, pressed from toasted sesame seeds, has a rich, nutty flavor. Look for it in well-stocked markets, health-food stores, and Asian groceries.

Corn Deep golden and relatively flavorless, this all-purpose oil is a good choice for deep-frying.

Olive Flavorful extra-virgin olive oil is made from the first pressing of the olives without the use of heat or chemicals. It is clear green or brownish and has a fruity, slightly peppery flavor that is used to best advantage when it will not be cooked. Olive oils extracted using heat or chemicals, then filtered and blended to eliminate much of the olives' character, may be used for general cooking. In the past, such oil was labeled "pure olive oil." Today, it is simply labeled "olive oil."

Peanut Pressed from peanuts, this oil has a hint of rich, nutty flavor. It can be used for deep-frying and to season marinades and dipping sauces.

Soybean This pale, all-purpose oil is pressed from soybeans. It has a pale color and a neutral flavor.

Walnut Rich-tasting and deep brown, walnut oil is used as a seasoning. It is not good for frying due to its low smoke point.

OLIVES
Olives are among the oldest and most important of the world's crops, especially throughout the Mediterranean, where they are prized for their oil or are cured.

Kalamata The most popular Greek variety, this almond-shaped olive is purplish black, rich, and meaty. It is brine cured and then packed in oil or vinegar.

Niçoise Small and brownish black, these mellow olives come from Provence. They are brine cured and then packed in oil.

ONIONS
This humble bulb vegetable, in the same family as leeks and garlic, is one of the most common ingredients in the kitchen.

Green Also known as scallions or spring onions, green onions are the immature shoots of the bulb onion, with a narrow white base and long, flat green leaves. They are mild in flavor.

Red These onions tend to be mild, slightly sweet, and purplish. They are delicious when used raw.

Yellow These are the familiar, all-purpose onions sold in supermarkets. Yellow onions are usually too harsh for serving raw, but they become rich and sweet when cooked.

OYSTERS These shellfish readily take on the flavor of their environments and are traditionally named after the area where they live. Atlantic oysters tend to have bumpy, elongated shells and a briny flavor. Pacific oysters, also known as Japanese oysters, have more subtle, slightly fruity flavors and more distinctly fluted shells. The sweet Kumamoto oyster is actually a separate species but is often grouped with the Pacific oysters. Flat oysters are native to European waters but now grow in both the Atlantic and Pacific. Varieties found in the waters off Maine and northern California are especially intense. They are commonly known by the name Belon. Buy oysters from reputable merchants who can vouch that they come from safe, unpolluted waters. Live oysters should have a mild, sweet smell; their shells should be closed and feel heavy with water.

PANCETTA This flavorful Italian bacon, which derives its name from *pancia*, the Italian word for "belly," has a moist, silky texture. It is made by rubbing a slab of pork belly with a simple mixture of spices, and then rolling the slab into a tight cylinder and curing it for at least 2 months.

PAPRIKA Red or orange-red, paprika is made from dried peppers. The finest paprikas come from Hungary and Spain in three basic grades: sweet, medium-sweet, and hot. The sweet types, which are mild but still pungent, are the most versatile.

PINE NUTS These small nuts have an elongated, slightly tapered shape and a delicate taste. Store them in an airtight container in a cool place away from light.

POMEGRANATE MOLASSES The sweet-sour concentrate of pomegranate juice, pomegranate molasses is used in Middle Eastern cooking. Purchase it at specialty-foods stores and Middle Eastern groceries.

PROSCIUTTO This Italian ham is a seasoned, salt-cured, air-dried rear leg of pork. Prosciutto is not smoked or cooked, and it is treated with a minimum of salt, but it is cured enough to be eaten without cooking. Aged from 10 months to 2 years, prosciutto from Parma in the Italian region of Emilia-Romagna is considered the best.

RADICCHIO This variety of Italian chicory is characterized by its variegated purplish red leaves. Its pleasantly bitter taste is a good match with other assertive ingredients.

RED PEPPER FLAKES The flakes and seeds that result from crushing dried red chiles. They are a popular seasoning in Italy, especially in the south, and just a pinch or two will add a bit of heat to a recipe.

SALMON A meaty, oily, firm fish prized for its flavorful, orange flesh. Salmon is best when it comes from the wild, not a farm, where it is weaned on additives and color enhancers and lacks good flavor. Wild salmon may harbor tiny roundworms that can cause illness unless the fish is cooked. Buy it from a top-quality merchant and always visually inspect it before using.

SALT Table salt is usually amended with iodine and with additives that enable it to flow freely. Kosher salt and sea salt are preferred by many cooks.

Kosher With a superior taste to table salt, kosher salt has large flakes that are easy to grasp. Since it is not as salty, kosher salt can be used more liberally than table salt.

Sea Available in coarse or fine grains, this salt is produced naturally by evaporation. It dissolves more readily than kosher salt.

SEEDS
Seeds play an important part in any spice pantry. Whether used whole or freshly ground, they add flavor, aroma, and texture.

Aniseed The seed of the anise plant, a member of the parsley family, aniseed has a licorice taste.

Coriander The dried ripe fruit of fresh coriander, or cilantro, these tiny, round, ridged seeds have an exotic flavor.

Cumin The seed of a member of the parsley family, cumin adds a sharp flavor to many Latin American and Indian dishes.

Fennel Used ground or whole, these elongated striped seeds add a licorice-like flavor to recipes.

Poppy Tiny in size, these dark seeds add crunch and a slight nutty flavor.

Sesame These tiny, flat seeds range in color from white to tan to black. Often toasted before adding to a dish, they contribute a nutty flavor and subtle texture.

SHALLOTS These small members of the onion family look like large cloves of garlic covered with papery bronze or reddish skin. Shallots have white flesh streaked with purple, a crisp texture, and a taste more subtle than that of onions.

SHRIMP Although often sold peeled and deveined, it's best to purchase shrimp (prawns) still in their shells if possible. Most shrimp have been previously frozen, and the shells help preserve their texture and flavor. To peel and devein shrimp at home, first pull off the head if it is still attached. Carefully pull off the legs on the inside of the curve of the shrimp. Starting at the head, carefully pull away the shell from the meat; pull off the tail too, unless otherwise directed. Using a paring knife, make a shallow cut down the back of each shrimp. With the tip of the knife, lift out and gently scrape away the dark veinlike intestinal tract.

STOCK A liquid derived from slowly simmering chicken, meat, fish, or vegetables along with herbs and aromatic ingredients such as onions in water. Stock can be made at home and frozen for future use. Good-quality canned broths are available, but they tend to be saltier than homemade stock. Seek out those labeled "low-sodium" or "reduced-sodium," so you can control the seasonings in your dish.

TAHINI This paste is made from ground sesame seeds and has a rich, creamy taste and a concentrated sesame flavor. It is popular in Middle Eastern cuisines.

TOMATILLOS These small green fruits look like small tomatoes, but they are actually relatives of the Cape gooseberry. They have a lemony, herbal flavor that plays an essential role in many Latin recipes, especially salsas.

Before using tomatillos, remove their parchmentlike skin and wash away any sticky residue.

TUNA Tuna is found in many forms, from canned albacore used for tuna salad to seared tuna steaks. Yellowfin tuna, also known as ahi, and bluefin tuna both boast deep red, meaty, firm, oily flesh that is ideal for making tartare (page 83).

VINEGAR
Many types are available, made from a variety of wines or, like rice vinegar, from grains. They often add just the right amount of tartness to a dish.

Balsamic This aged vinegar is made from the unfermented grape juice of white Trebbiano grapes. Balsamic is aged for as little as 1 year or for as long as 75 years; the vinegar slowly evaporates and grows sweeter and mellower.

Champagne This light, delicate vinegar is more subtle than other white wine vinegars. Use it to add just a bit of acidity.

Rice Produced from fermented rice, this vinegar adds a slight acidity to dishes. It is available unseasoned or sweetened; the latter is labeled "seasoned rice vinegar."

Sherry This full-bodied vinegar, originally from Spain, has a full, nutty taste.

Wine Common pantry staples, red or white wine vinegar is created when wine is allowed to ferment naturally over a period of months.

WASABI Similar to horseradish, this pungent Japanese root is commonly sold as a green powder that can be reconstituted with water. It adds a pungent taste to any dish.

WATERCRESS Characterized by a refreshing peppery flavor, watercress has an agreeably assertive taste like many other members of the mustard family. Remove and discard the thick stems and rinse and dry the leaves well before using.

WHITE PEPPER Made from black peppercorns that have had their skins removed before the berries are dried, white pepper is often less aromatic and milder in flavor than black pepper. It is favored in the preparation of light-colored dishes.

Index

FREE PRESS

A Division of Simon & Schuster, Inc.
1230 Avenue of the Americas
New York, NY 10020

WILLIAMS-SONOMA

Founder & Vice-Chairman Chuck Williams

WELDON OWEN INC.

Chief Executive Officer John Owen
President and Chief Operating Officer Terry Newell
Chief Financial Officer Christine E. Munson
Vice President International Sales Stuart Laurence
Creative Director Gaye Allen
Publisher Hannah Rahill
Senior Editor Jennifer Newens
Editor Heather Belt
Editorial Assistant Juli Vendzules
Art Director Kyrie Forbes
Designers Marisa Kwek and Adrienne Aquino
Production Director Chris Hemesath
Color Manager Teri Bell
Production and Reprint Coordinator Todd Rechner
Food Stylist Alison Attenborough
Prop Stylist Leigh Nöe
Assistant Food Stylists Ann Belden, Jen Carden, and Katie Christ
Assistant Food Stylist and Hand Model Brittany Williams
Photographer's Assistant Mark Jordan

PHOTO CREDITS

Bill Bettencourt, all photography, except the following:
Mark Thomas: Pages 12 (center and right),
43 (juicing citrus sequence), and 133 (top far right).
Jeff Kauck: Page 114 (bottom far left).

THE MASTERING SERIES

Conceived and produced by Weldon Owen Inc.
814 Montgomery Street, San Francisco, CA 94133
Telephone: 415 291 0100 Fax: 415 291 8841

In collaboration with Williams-Sonoma, Inc.
3250 Van Ness Avenue, San Francisco, CA 94109

A WELDON OWEN PRODUCTION
Copyright © 2005 by Weldon Owen Inc. and Williams-Sonoma Inc.

All rights reserved, including the right of reproduction in whole or in part
in any form.

FREE PRESS and colophon are registered trademarks of Simon & Schuster, Inc.

For information regarding special discounts for bulk purchases,
please contact Simon & Schuster Special Sales at 1 800 456 6798 or
business@simonandschuster.com

Set in ITC Berkeley and FF The Sans.

Color separations by Embassy Graphics.
Printed and bound in China by SNP Leefung Printers Limited.

First printed in 2005.

10 9 8 7 6 5 4 3 2 1

Library of Congress Cataloging-in-Publication data is available.

ISBN–13: 978-0-7432-6738-0
ISBN–10: 0-7432-6738-9

ACKNOWLEDGMENTS

Weldon Owen wishes to thank the following people for their
generous support in producing this book: Desne Ahlers,
Ken DellaPenta, Emily Jahn, Ashley Johnson, Karen Kemp,
Rachel Koryl, M. Bridget Maley, Tracy Marcuzzi, Cynthia Scheer,
Laura Shear, Sharon Silva, Bob Simmons, Coleen Simmons,
Lindsay Walsh, and Tsar Nicoulai Caviar for donating the caviar
that appears on pages 5, 76, and 81.

A NOTE ON WEIGHTS AND MEASURES

All recipes include customary U.S. and metric measurements. Metric conversions are based on
a standard developed for these books and have been rounded off. Actual weights may vary.